SPANISH HERITAGE DICTIONARY

ÉDITIONS RÉNYI INC.

355 Adelaide Street West, Suite 400, Toronto, Ontario Canada M5V 1S2

Spanish Heritage Dictionary

Copyright © 1989 Éditions Rényi Inc.

Illustrated by Kathryn Adams, Pat Gangnon, Colin Gilles, David Shaw and Yvonne Zan

Designed by David Shaw and Associates

Cover illustration by Colin Gilles

Colour separations by New Concept Limited

Printed in Singapore

Typesetting by Osgoode Technical Translations

English language editors: P. O'Brien-Hitching, R. LeBel, P. Renyi, K.C. Sheppard

Spanish edition by P. Mason, L. Garcia

Spanish Heritage Dictionary   ISBN 0-921606-36-2

INTRODUCTION

Some of Canada's best illustrators have contributed to this dictionary, which has been carefully designed to appeal to children, so that learning new words can be a pleasure.

Its unusually large number of terms – 3336 – makes the dictionary a flexible teaching tool. Because the vocabulary it encompasses is so broad, this dictionary can also be used to teach English as a Second Language to older children and adults, as well as helping young children acquire language skills.

NOTE TO TEACHERS AND PARENTS

In a children's dictionary, the most difficult decision is usually which words to include and which ones to leave out. Here, word selection has been based partly on word frequency analysis of English usage (in order to include the most commonly used terms), and partly on thematic clustering (in order to cover major fields of activity or interest).

This process was further complicated by the decision to systematically illustrate the meanings. Although the degree of abstraction has been kept reasonably low, it was deemed necessary to include terms such as "to expect" and "to forgive", which are virtually impossible to illustrate, given the space and other constraints. Instead of dropping these words, we decided to provide explanatory sentences that create a context.

Where variations occur between British and North-American English, both terms are given with an asterisk marking the British version (favor/favour*, gas/petrol*). Both variants are listed alphabetically in the index.

The alphabetical index at the end of the book lists every term in the dictionary with the number of its corresponding illustration. Teachers could use this feature to expand children's numeracy skills, by asking the child to match an index number with the actual illustration, as well as using it to train students in dictionary skills.

Great care has been taken to ensure that any contextual statements made are factual, have some educational value and are compatible with statements made elsewhere in the book. Lastly, from a strictly psychological viewpoint, the little girl featured in the book has not been made into a paragon of virtue; children will readily identify with her imperfections.

A todos mis amigos

A lo mejor éste sea el primer diccionario de verdad que van a tener. ¡Ojalá que les guste tanto como me gusta a mí!

Yo me llamo Marisol, soy una niñita, voy a la escuela y a clases de natación. Tengo un hermanito menor y un montón de opiniones sobre un montón de cosas. Mi papá es un almirante, y si quieren conocerlo, allá se ve, en la página siguiente. El está justo en la parte de abajo. ¿Lo ven? Mi mamá aparece en la página que viene después, arriba, a la derecha. Y si quieren conocerme a mí, búsquenme en la palabra "calmada".

En este viaje que vamos a hacer juntos ustedes aprenderán muchas palabras útiles e interesantes, y algunos números también.

Cinco personas grandes se entretuvieron de lo lindo haciendo los dibujos que encontrarán en todo el libro. Uno de ellos lo hice yo (una cebra). ¿Vieron ya con qué palabra termina el diccionario?

Bueno, este libro se hizo especialmente y con mucho cariño para mis amiguitos, y yo espero que a todos les guste mucho.

Marisol

el ábaco

1   abacus

acerca de, a punto de

Cuéntame más **acerca de** eso.
Estoy **a punto de** partir.

Tell me about it.
I'm about to leave.

2   about

Tiene la manzana **por encima** de la cabeza.

3   above

Jorge está **ausente**.

4   absent

Todo automóvil tiene **un acelerador**.

5   accelerator

el acento

Jacques habla con **acento** francés.
Ponga **el acento** sobre la primera sílaba.

Jacques speaks with a French accent.
Put the accent on the first syllable.

6   accent

el accidente

7   accident

el acordeón

8   accordion

Todos **acusaron** a Georgina.

9   to accuse

¿Cuántos **ases** tiene la baraja?

10   ace

Me **duele** la cabeza.

11   My head **aches**.

El ácido quema la piel.

12   acid

De **la bellota** nace el roble.

13   acorn

la acróbata

14   acrobat

enfrente, de un extremo al otro

Jorge vive **enfrente**.
He viajado **de un extremo al otro** del país.

Jorge lives across the street.
I have travelled across the country.

15   across

Suma estas cantidades.

16   to add

Esta es **la dirección** de Marisol.

17   address

El papá de Marisol es **almirante.**

18   admiral

Yo te **adoro**.

19   to adore

Los adultos son personas grandes.

20   adult

avanzar

21   to advance

¿Es **una ventaja** ser alto?

22   advantage

A la mamá de Marisol le encanta **la aventura**.

23   adventure

Belisario está muy **asustado**.

24   He is **afraid**.

Africa es un continente.

25   Africa

después de, perseguir, tras

Puedes jugar **después de** la comida.
Ella me **persigue**.
¡Vé **tras** la pelota!

You can play after dinner.
She's after me.
Go after the ball!

26   after

La tarde empieza después del mediodía.

27   afternoon

otra vez, más

¡El partido va a empezar **otra vez**!
No lo vuelvas a hacer nunca **más**.

The game is starting again!
Don't do it ever again.

28   again

A Micifuz le gusta restregarse **contra** mis pantalones.

29   to rub **against**

¡Qué gran diferencia de **edades**!

30   age

Los atletas son personas muy **ágiles**.

31   **agile** person

un barco **encallado**

32   aground

adelante de, por adelantado

Rosita se sienta **adelante de** Martín.
Avisa tu llegada **por adelantado**.

Rosita sits ahead of Martin.
Call ahead to tell them you're coming.

33   ahead

ayudar

34   to provide **aid**

¿Estás **apuntando** bien?

35   to aim

La cometa se remonta por **los aires**.

36   air

el colchón inflable

37   air mattress

Hay un insecto en la campana **hermética**.

38   airtight

A este **avión** le pasa algo.

39   airplane/aeroplane*

Los aviones aterrizan en **el aeropuerto**.

40 airport

Tu butaca está junto al **pasillo**.

41 aisle

el despertador

42 alarm clock

Este es mi **álbum** de fotografías.

43 album

¡La casa está **en llamas**!

44 alight

Este está **vivo** y coleando.

45 alive

Los quiero **todos**.

46 I want them **all**.

Este es un gatito de **callejón**.

47 alley

el caimán

48 alligator

la almendra

49 almond

Este perrito **casi**, **casi** muerde el hueso.

50 almost

No entiendo por qué se sienta **solo**.

51 alone

¡Ven **conmigo**!

52 along

en **voz alta, fuerte**

53 aloud

las letras del **alfabeto**

a b c ch d e f g h
i j k l ll m n ñ o
p q r s t u v w x y z
A B C D CH D E F G H I J
K L LL M N Ñ O P Q R S T U
V W X Y Z

54 alphabet

¿**Ya** me tengo que ir?

55 Do I have to go **already?**

Me duele un poco, pero **estoy bien**.

56 I am **alright**.

Yo **también** quiero un poco.

57 I **also** want some.

la escalera de **aluminio**

58 aluminum/aluminium* ladder

Siempre me estoy cayendo.

59 I **always** fall down.

la ambulancia	un lobo **entre** las ovejas	**el ancla**	unos restos **antiguos**
60 ambulance	61 wolf **among** sheep	62 anchor	63 ancient
el ángulo	Malandrín está **enojado**.	**los animales**	**el tobillo**
64 angle	65 He is **angry**.	66 animals	67 ankle
anunciar	**otro** sandwich	y **la respuesta** es . . .	**la hormiga**
68 to **announce**	69 **another** sandwich	70 The **answer** is...	71 ant
la Antártida	**el antílope**	**los cuernos, las astas, la cornamenta**	No tengo **nada** de dinero.
72 Antarctic	73 antelope	74 . antlers	75 I do not have **any** money.
Las cabras se comen **cualquier cosa**.	Malandrín está enojado porque no puede salir a **ninguna parte**.	Una de las uvas está **separada** del racimo.	**el simio**
76 It eats **anything**.	77 He cannot go **anywhere**.	78 apart	79 ape

la abejera, el colmenar

80   apiary

disculparse, disculpar

Disculparse es casi lo mismo que pedir perdón. Quiero que me disculpen por llegar atrasado.

To apologize means to say you are sorry.
I apologize for being late!

81   to apologize/apologise*

aparecer, parecer

Apareció de la nada.
Parece que está nevando.
La Reina apareció en la televisión.

He appeared out of nowhere.
It appears to be snowing.
The Queen appeared on television.

82   to appear

aplaudir

83   to applaud

la manzana

84   apple

el corazón de manzana

85   apple core

acercarse, aproximarse

86   to approach

el damasco, el albaricoque

87   apricot

En abril, lluvias mil.

88   April

el delantal

89   apron

el acuario

90   aquarium

el arco

91   arch

el arquitecto

92   architect

En el Ártico hace mucho frió.

93   Arctic

discutir

94   to argue

el brazo

95   arm

el sillón

96   armchair

El Cid Campeador usaba armadura.

97   armor/armour*

la axila, el sobaco

98   armpit

dar la vuelta a, cerca de, alrededor de

La vuelta al mundo en ochenta días
A la función llegaron cerca de cien personas.
Toti llega a casa alrededor del mediodía.

Around the world in eighty days
The show attracted around one hundred people.
Toti comes home around noon.

99   around

A Jorge le gusta **arreglar** flores.	La policía **arrestó** a Malandrín.	**llegar**	**la flecha**
100 to **arrange** flowers	101 to **arrest**	102 to **arrive**	103 arrow
la alcachofa	**el artista**	**tan . . . como, en cuanto a, tal como** **Tan** pronto **como** tú quieras. **En cuanto a** ti, te has metido en un problema. **Tal como** te iba diciendo . . . *As soon as you like.* *As for you, I think you are in trouble!* *As I was saying . . .*	**la ceniza**
104 artichoke	105 artist	106 as	107 ash
el cenicero	**Asia** es un continente.	**Preguntemos** cómo llegar.	Pilar y Micifuz se quedaron **dormidos**.
108 ashtray	109 Asia	110 to **ask** for directions	111 asleep
los espárragos	Toma dos **aspirinas** para el dolor de cabeza.	Matilde **se asombra** de todo.	**el astronauta**
112 asparagus	113 aspirin	114 to **astonish**	115 astronaut
el astrónomo	**en, al, por** Rosita está **en** casa con su papá. **Al** principio no podía escuchar. **Por** lo menos me trajo flores. *Rosita is at home with her dad.* *At first I couldn't hear.* *At least he brought me flowers.*	**la atleta**	**el atlas**
116 astronomer	117 at	118 athlete	119 atlas

la atmósfera de la Tierra	**el átomo**	**unir, juntar**	¡Presta **atención**!
120　atmosphere	121　atom	122　to attach	123　Pay attention!
¿Qué cosas se guardan en **el desván**?	**el público**	En el hemisferio norte hace calor en **agosto**.	Mi **tía** es la hermana de mi mamá.
124　attic	125　audience	126　August	127　My aunt is my mother's sister.
Australia es una isla-continente.	**el autor, el escritor, el compositor**	un despertador **automático**	**el otoño**
128　Australia	129　author	130　automatic	131　autumn
la avalancha	**la palta, el aguacate**	¿Cómo es que todavía estás **despierto**?	Ella **no está**.
132　avalanche	133　avocado	134　awake	135　She is away.
un olor **atroz**	una persona **torpe, desgarbada**	**el hacha**	Un **eje** conecta dos ruedas.
136　an awful smell	137　an awkward person	138　axe	139　axle

B

el bebé, el nene, la criatura

140   baby

el cochecito para bebés

141   baby carriage/pram*

Ráscame **la espalda**, por favor.

142   back

tocino con huevos

144   bacon and eggs

la manzana estaba **mala**

145   bad apple

la insignia, el distintivo

146   badge

retroceder

143   to back up

¿Qué hay en esta **bolsa**?

147   bag

El queso es el mejor **cebo** para cazar ratones.

148   bait

hornear, cocer

149   to bake

el panadero

150   baker

la panadería

151   bakery

un muy buen **equilibrio**

152   good balance

el balcón

153   balcony

Raúl es **calvo**.

154   bald

la pelota, el balón

155   ball

la bailarina

156   ballerina

la función de **ballet**

157   ballet

el globo

158   balloon

el globo aerostático

159　hot air **balloon**

el plátano, la banana, el guineo

160　**banana**

la cinta para el pelo, el cintillo

161　**band**

el grupo musical

162　musical **band**

El doctor me puso este **vendaje**.

163　**bandage**

golpear, batir

164　to **bang**

la baranda, el pasamanos

165　**banister**

En **el banco** se guarda el dinero.

166　**bank**

la barra

167　**bar**

Los bares son para las personas grandes.

168　**bar/pub***

la alambrada de púas

169　**barbed wire**

Ignacio fue al **peluquero**.

170　**barber**

un pie **descalzo**

171　one **bare** foot

¡A ese precio es una verdadera **ganga**!

172　**bargain**

la barcaza, el lanchón

173　**barge**

ladrar

174　to **bark**

La cebada crece en el campo.

176　**barley**

el granero

177　**barn**

Los soldados viven en **los cuarteles**.

178　**barracks**

la corteza

175　**bark**

el barril de aceite

179   barrel

el cañón de una pistola

180   barrel

la traba, el pasador

181   barrette/hair slide*

la barrera

182   barrier

la base de una columna

183   base

la base de béisbol

184   base

el béisbol

185   baseball

el sótano, el subterráneo

186   basement/cellar*

la albahaca

187   basil

la canasta, la cesta

188   basket

la pelota de baloncesto

189   basketball

los bates de béisbol y criquet

190   bats

Me estoy dando **un baño**.

192   I am having a **bath**.

la sala de baño, el cuarto de baño, el baño

193   bathroom

la tina, la bañera

194   bathtub

Los murciélagos vuelan de noche.

191   bat

Me hace falta **una pila** para mi radio.

195   battery

la bahía

196   bay

Mi mamá cocina con hojas de **laurel**.

197   bay leaves

el bazar

198   bazaar

ser, estar

Yo **soy** buen alumno.
Voy a **estar** fuera por unos días.
Marisol, ¿dónde **está** Martín?

I am a good student.
I am going to be away for a few days.
Marisol, where is Martin?

199   to **be**

la playa

200   **beach**

un collar de **cuentas**

201   **bead**

el pico de un loro

202   **beak**

el rayo, el haz de luz

203   **beam** of light

los porotos, los frijoles, las judías, las habichuelas

204   **beans**

Este **oso** sabe andar en bicicleta.

205   **bear**

Don Manuel tiene **una barba** muy larga.

206   **beard**

¡Qué **bestia** más horrible!

207   **beast**

Hilda **toca** el tambor.

208   to **beat**

una perrita **hermosa**

209   **beautiful**

El castor construye diques.

210   **beaver**

Estoy llorando **porque** . . .

211   I am crying **because...**

convertirse

La oruga

se convierte

en mariposa.

212   to **become**

Ya es hora de irse a **la cama.**

213   **bed**

la lámpara de cabecera

214 bed lamp/reading light*

el dormitorio

215   **bedroom**

La abeja es un insecto muy útil.

216   **bee**

el haya

217   **beech**

Las abejas viven en **colmenas.**

218   **beehive**

la jarra de **cerveza**
219 beer

la remolacha, la betarraga
220 beet/beet root*

el escarabajo
221 beetle

Lávate las manos **antes de** comer.
222 Wash your hands **before** dinner.

mendigar, pordiosear
223 to beg

empezar, comenzar, iniciarse
Para **empezar**, tomemos el desayuno.
La clase de piano de Marisol **comienza** a las diez.
Las clases **se inician** en marzo.

To begin with, let's have breakfast! Marisol's piano lesson begins at ten o'clock. School begins in March.

224 to **begin**

Eliana **se porta** muy bien.
225 to behave

Leonor está escondida **detrás** del árbol.
226 behind

beige
227 beige

Yo **creo** que los dragones sí existen.
228 I **believe** in dragons.

la campana
229 bell

el ombligo
230 belly button

Este perrito **me pertenece** a mí.
231 He **belongs** to me.

El gato está **debajo** de la mesa.
232 below

el cinturón
233 belt

el **banco** de la plaza
234 bench

el recodo en el camino
235 bend

doblar
236 to bend

la boina
237 beret

Carmen está **al lado del** árbol.
238 beside

además de, además

¿No crees que **además del** postre deberías comer otra cosa?
Además, te hace mal tanta azúcar.

Should you not eat something else besides dessert?
Besides, you should not eat so much sugar.

239　　besides

la mejor

240　　best

mejor, más vale

Daniela escribe **mejor** que Esteban.
Más vale tarde que nunca.

Daniela writes better than Esteban.
Better late than never.

241　　better

Felipe pasa **entre** las rocas.

242　　between

el babero

243　　bib

la bicicleta

244　　bicycle

grande

245　　big

Una **bici** es lo mismo que una bicicleta.

246　　bike

el billete

247　　bill/banknote*

el cartel

248　　billboard/hoarding*

El **billar** es un juego de salón.

249　　billiards/snooker*

atar, amarrar

250　　to bind/tie up*

los binoculares, los prismáticos, los gemelos

251　　binoculars

el pájaro, el ave

252　　bird

el nacimiento

Yo soy canadiense de **nacimiento**.
¿Tú tienes un certificado de **nacimiento**?
Indica tu lugar de **nacimiento**.

I am a Canadian by birth.
Do you have a birth certificate?
State your place of birth.

253　　birth

¡Feliz **cumpleaños**!

254　　birthday

la galleta, el bizcocho

255　　biscuit

Los dientes sirven para **morder**.

256　　to bite

Saqué **un mordisco** grande.

257　　bite

amargo

La cerveza tiene un sabor **amargo**.
Marisol lloró amargamente cuando se le perdió su muñeca preferida.

Beer has a bitter taste.
Marisol shed bitter tears when she lost her favorite doll.

258　　bitter

negro

259   black

la mora

260   blackberry

el mirlo

261   blackbird

Martín hizo un dibujo en **la pizarra**.

262   blackboard

la grosella, el casis

263   blackcurrant

el herrero

264   blacksmith

la hoja de la espada

265   blade

echar la culpa, tener la culpa

El papá le **echó la culpa** a Marisol, pero no fue ella quien lo hizo.
El que **tiene la culpa** es Luis.

Dad blamed Marisol, but she did not do it.
Luis is to blame.

266   to blame

una hoja **en blanco**

267   blank page

la frazada, la manta

268   blanket

Un estallido es lo mismo que una explosión.

269   blast

hacer volar, hacer estallar

270   to blast

Los bomberos apagaron **el incendio**.

271   blaze

la chaqueta, la americana

272   blazer

El blanqueador sirve para limpiar la ropa.

273   bleach

Me está **sangrando** la nariz.

274   to bleed

la licuadora

275   blender

Los ciegos no pueden ver.

276   blind

pestañear, parpadear

277   to blink

Las ampollas duelen mucho.

278   blister

la tempestad de nieve

279   blizzard

¿Tú juegas con cubos?

280   block

la manzana, la cuadra

281   block

La policía le cerró el paso a Gabriel.

282   to block

la cabellera rubia

283   blond/blonde*

la transfusión de sangre

284   blood

la planta en flor

285   bloom

florecer

286   to blossom

la mancha de tinta

287   blot

la blusa

288   blouse

un golpe en la cabeza

289   a **blow** to the head

soplar

290   to blow

azul

291   blue

el arándano

292   blueberries

romo, brusco

Este cuchillo está **romo** y no sirve para cortar tomates.
Eliana fue muy **brusca** con él.

This knife is too blunt to cut the tomato.
Eliana was very blunt with him.

293   blunt

Isabel se ruboriza con facilidad.

294   to blush

el jabalí

295   boar

el tablero

296   board

jactarse, ufanarse

A Cristóbal le gusta **jactarse**.
De lo que más **se ufana** es de su modestia.

Cristobal likes to boast.
His modesty is nothing to boast about.

297   to boast

el bote

298   boat

la horquilla

299　bobby pin/hairgrip*

el cuerpo humano

300　body

hervir

301　to boil

el perno

302　bolt

¡A otro perro con ese **hueso**!

303　bone

la fogata, la hoguera

304　bonfire

el libro

305　book

el estante, la repisa para libros

306　bookshelf

el bumerang

307　boomerang

la bota

308　boot

Esta es **la frontera** entre dos países.

309　border

Es difícil **horadar** el cemento.

310　to bore

nacer

¿En qué año **naciste**?
Los niños **nacen** para ser felices.

What year were you born?
Children are born to be happy.

312　born

pedir prestado, tomar prestado

¿Te podría **pedir prestado** algo de dinero?
A veces, Marisol **toma prestada** la bicicleta de su hermano.

Can I borrow some money?
Marisol often borrows her brother's bike.

313　to borrow

el jefe

314　boss

aburrir

A veces, Marisol **aburre** a la gente.
Tomás **me aburre** porque habla demasiado.

Sometimes, Marisol bores people.
Tomas bores me because he talks too much.

311　to bore

los dos, ambos

Los dos vamos a ir.
Pruébate **ambos** zapatos.

Both you and I are going.
Try on both shoes.

315　both

la botella, el frasco

316　bottle

el abridor

317　bottle opener

el fondo

318　bottom

la roca

319   boulder

La pelota **rebotó**
en el suelo.

320   to bounce

**el ramillete,
el ramo** de flores

321   bouquet

---

arco y flecha

322   bow

---

el tazón, el bol

324   bowl

¿Qué hay dentro de
la caja?

325   box

---

el boxeador, el pugilista

326   boxer

**la pajarita, el corbatín, la corbata
de lazo o de humita**

323   bow tie

---

el niño

327   boy

---

el sostén

328   bra

---

la pulsera, el brazalete

329   bracelet

---

presumir, fanfarronear

María **presume** de
sus juguetes nuevos.
Su papá le dice que no hay
que **fanfarronear**.

*Maria brags about her
new toys.
Her dad tells her not to brag.*

330   to brag

---

el cerebro

331   brain

Todo automóvil tiene
frenos.

332   brake

---

frenar

333   to brake

---

la rama del árbol

334   branch

---

valiente

El dentista dice que tú eres
muy **valiente**.

*The dentist says you are
very brave.*

335   brave

---

el pan

336   bread

---

romper, quebrar

337   to break

**descomponerse, echarse
a perder, fallar**

338   to break down

Un ladrón **entró a robar**.	**el desayuno**	mal **aliento**	**respirar**
339 to break in	340 breakfast	341 breath	342 to breathe
Mi casa está hecha de **ladrillos**.	Gabriela trabaja como **albañil**.	**La novia** es tímida.	Y **el novio** también.
343 brick	344 bricklayer	345 bride	346 bridegroom
el puente	Los caballos llevan **bridas**.	**el maletín, la cartera, el portafolio**	El sol está muy **brillante**.
347 bridge	348 bridle	349 briefcase	350 bright sun
Macabeo me **trae** las zapatillas.	Marisol viene a **devolver** libros a la biblioteca.	vidrio **quebradizo**	**el brécol, el bróculi, el brócoli**
351 to bring	352 to bring back	353 brittle glass	354 broccoli
el broche, el prendedor	**Un arroyo** es un río pequeño.	**la escoba**	Yo quiero mucho a mi **hermano**.
355 brooch	356 brook	357 broom	358 I love my brother.

las cejas, la frente	**marrón, café**	A Daniel le hace falta **cepillarse** el pelo.	**el cepillo, la escobilla**
359 brow	360 brown	362 to brush	363 brush
la herida, el golpe, la magulladura	**los repollitos, la col de Bruselas**	**la brocha, el pincel**	**el cepillo de dientes**
361 bruise	366 brussels sprouts	364 paintbrush	365 toothbrush
la burbuja	**el cubo, el balde, la cubeta**	**la hebilla**	**el capullo, el botón, el brote, el cogollo**
367 bubble	368 bucket	369 belt buckle	370 bud
el búfalo, el bisonte	**el bicho, la sabandija**	**la corneta, el clarín**	**construir, edificar**
371 buffalo	372 bug	373 bugle	374 to build
el toro	**la excavadora, la niveladora, el buldozer**	**Las balas** son muy peligrosas.	**el megáfono, el altoparlante**
375 bull	376 bulldozer	377 bullet	378 bullhorn/megaphone*

Javier es **un matón**.

379   bully

el chichón

380   bump

los parachoques

381   bumpers

el manojo de espárragos

382   bunch

el atado

383   bundle

la boya, la baliza

384   buoy

el ladrón

385   burglar

El fuego **ardió** con rapidez.

386   to burn

El globo **se reventó**.

387   to burst

enterrar, sepultar

388   to bury

el autobús, el bus, el ómnibus

389   bus

la parada de autobús, el paradero

390   bus stop

Un arbusto es más pequeño que un árbol.

391   bush

Ahora estoy **ocupado**.

392   I am **busy** now.

pero, sino

Me gustaría ir, **pero** estoy ocupado.
Hoy no es lunes, **sino** martes.

I would like to go, but I am busy.
Today is not Monday, but Tuesday.

393   but

el carnicero

394   butcher

¿Quieres pan con **mantequilla**?

395   butter

la mariposa

396   butterfly

tres **botones**

397   buttons

Felipe **compra** un helado.

398   to buy

el repollo, la col

399   cabbage

una cabaña en el bosque

400   cabin

la cómoda, el armario

401   cabinet

el cable

402   cable/lead*

el cacto, el cactus

403   cactus

la jaula

404   cage

el pastel, la torta

405   cake

el calculador, la calculadora

406   calculator

el calendario, el almanaque

407   calendar

el ternero, el becerro

408   calf

llamar

409   to **call**

Marisol se ve siempre muy **calmada.**

412   She is **calm.**

el camello

413   camel

la cámara, la máquina fotográfica

414   camera

suspender, cancelar

Si llueve vamos a **suspender** el paseo.
Marisol **canceló** la visita al zoológico.

We will call off the picnic if it rains.
Marisol has called off our trip to the zoo.

410   to **call off**

Mi papá y yo salimos a **acampar.**

415   to **camp**

el campamento

416   campsite

la lata, el bote, el tarro

417   can

llamar por teléfono, telefonear

411   to **call up**/to **phone***

el abrelatas

418 can opener/tin* opener

Los barcos pasan por **el canal**.

419   canal

el canario

420   canary

la vela

421   candle

la palmatoria

422   candlestick

los caramelos

423   candy/sweets*

El bastón sirve de apoyo al caminar.

424   cane/walking stick*

el cañón

425   cannon

No puedo ver nada.

426   I cannot see.

la canoa

427   canoe

el melón

428   cantaloupe

El río corre por el fondo del **cañón**.

429   canyon

la gorra, el gorro

430   cap

¿Dónde queda **el Cabo de Hornos**?

431   cape

aventuras de **capa** y espada.

432   cape

una letra **mayúscula**

N

433   capital

Este es **el capitán** del barco.

434   captain

capturar, atrapar

435   to capture

el automóvil, el coche, el carro

436   car

La caravana cruza el desierto.

437   caravan

los naipes, las cartas

438   cards

el cartón

439   cardboard

Las enfermeras **cuidan** a los enfermos

440   to care

Este es un niño **descuidado**.

441   He is careless.

la carga

442   cargo

los claveles

443   carnation

Un carnaval es una fiesta muy grande.

444   carnival

la carpintera

445   carpenter

la alfombra, el tapiz, el tapete

446   carpet

el carrito, el cochecito

447   carriage/pram*

la zanahoria

448   carrot

El Sr. Martínez **lleva** una carga muy pesada.

449   to carry

el carretón, la carreta

450   cart

la caja de cartón

451   carton

trinchar

452   to carve

la caja

453   case

Tener **plata** es lo mismo que tener dinero.

454   cash

las castañas de cajú, las nueces de acajú

455   cashew nuts

el castillo

456   castle

el gato

457   cat

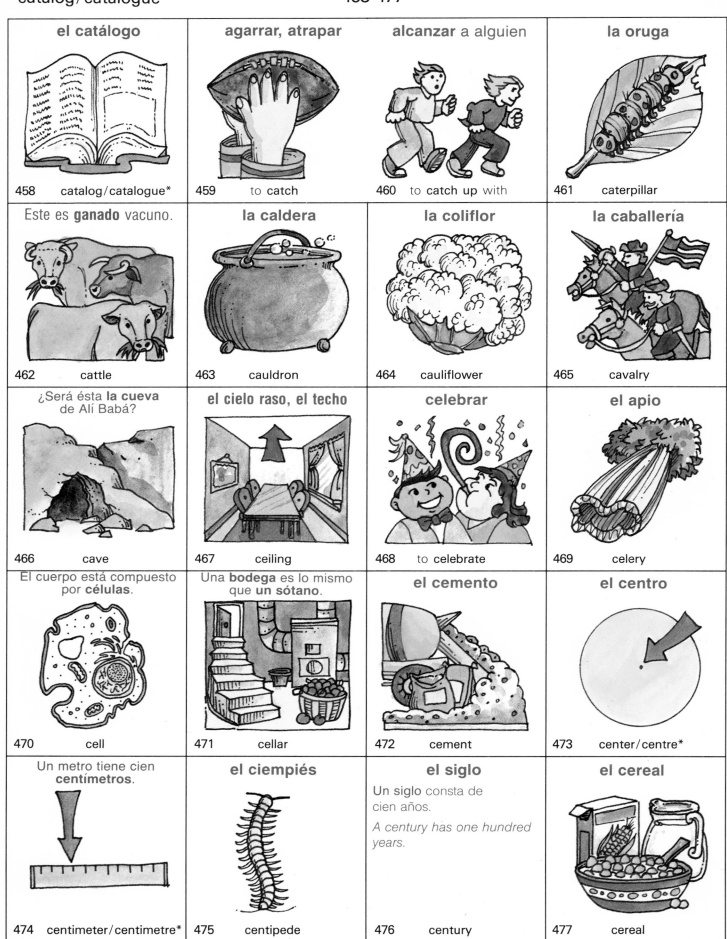

el catálogo	**agarrar, atrapar**	**alcanzar** a alguien	**la oruga**
458 catalog/catalogue*	459 to catch	460 to catch up with	461 caterpillar
Este es **ganado** vacuno.	**la caldera**	**la coliflor**	**la caballería**
462 cattle	463 cauldron	464 cauliflower	465 cavalry
¿Será ésta **la cueva** de Alí Babá?	**el cielo raso, el techo**	**celebrar**	**el apio**
466 cave	467 ceiling	468 to celebrate	469 celery
El cuerpo está compuesto por **células**.	Una **bodega** es lo mismo que **un sótano**.	**el cemento**	**el centro**
470 cell	471 cellar	472 cement	473 center/centre*
Un metro tiene cien **centímetros**.	**el ciempiés**	**el siglo** Un siglo consta de cien años. *A century has one hundred years.*	**el cereal**
474 centimeter/centimetre*	475 centipede	476 century	477 cereal

seguro, cierto

Marisol está **segura** de tener la razón.
Marcelo le causó **cierta** impresión.

Marisol is certain that she is right.
She has a certain feeling about Marcelo.

478 certain

el certificado

479 certificate

la cadena

480 chain

la sierra de cadena, la motosierra

481 chainsaw

la silla

482 chair

la tiza

483 chalk

la campeona

484 champion

el cambio, el vuelto, el sencillo

485 change

el canal

487 channel

Este libro tiene varios **capítulos**

488 chapter

el carácter, el personaje

Marisol tiene **un carácter** muy fuerte.
Ella es todo **un personaje**.
¿Qué quiere decir este **carácter**?

Marisol has a strong character.
She is quite a character.
What does this character mean?

489 character

Raúl **se cambió** de ropa.

486 to change

el carbón

490 charcoal

la acelga

491 chard

formular cargos, cargar

La policía **formuló cargos** de robo en contra de Malandrín.
Tu juguete dejó de funcionar porque se me olvidó **cargarle** las pilas.

The police charged Malandrin with robbery.
Your toy has stopped because I forgot to charge the battery.

492 to charge

la cuadriga

493 chariot

el gráfico

494 chart

perseguir

495 to chase

charlar

496 to chat

un lápiz **barato** y una corona cara

497 **cheap** pencil, expensive crown

César está tratando de **hacer trampa.**	**revisar, dejar** ¿**Revisaste** tus tareas antes de entregarlas? **Deje** el abrigo a la entrada, por favor. *Did you check your homework before handing it in? Check your coat at the entrance, please.*	**la mejilla**	**El queso** se hace a partir de la leche.
498 to cheat	499 to check	500 cheek	501 cheese
el cheque	**las cerezas, las guindas**	a lo hecho, **pecho**	**la castaña**
502 cheque*/check	503 cherries	504 chest	505 chestnut
Mastica bien antes de tragar.	**los garbanzos**	**el pollo, la polla**	**la varicela**
506 to chew	507 chick peas	508 chicken	509 chicken-pox
el comandante en **jefe**	**la niña**	un día **helado**	**la chimenea**
510 chief	511 child	512 a chilly day	513 chimney
el chimpancé	**el mentón, la barbilla**	**la vajilla de porcelana**	de tal palo, tal **astilla**
514 chimpanzee	515 chin	516 china/crockery*	517 chip

El escultor talla con **un cincel**.

518   chisel

**las cebolletas,
los cebollines**

519   chives

la barra de **chocolate**

520   chocolate

¿Te gusta cantar a **coro**?

521   choir

Ahogar a alguien es pésima broma.

522   to choke

Pedro **se atoró** con un hueso de pollo.

523   to choke on

Quisiera **escoger** uno de éstos.

524   to choose

Picar cebollas hace llorar.

525   to chop

los palillos chinos

526   chopsticks

el cromado del parachoques

527   chrome

el crisantemo

528   chrysanthemum

el trozo de carbón

529   a chunk/lump* of coal

Los puros son hediondos.

530   cigar

Los cigarrillos hacen muy mal.

531   cigarette

el círculo

532   circle

el circo

533   circus

Yo vivo en **una ciudad**.

534   city

Las almejas viven en su concha.

535   clam

tablas sujetas con **grapa**

536   clamp

aplaudir, batir palmas

537   to clap

la sala de clases, el aula

538   classroom

Los cangrejos tienen unas **pinzas** grandes.

539   claw

---

la arcilla, la greda

La arcilla se usa para hacer ladrillos.
Con la greda se pueden hacer ollas y platos.

Clay is used to make bricks.
You can also make pots and dishes out of clay.

540   clay

Ella está **limpia**, él está sucio.

541   She is all **clean.**

La tía Julia **levanta** la mesa.

542   to clear

---

el acantilado

543   cliff

Vamos **escalando** hacia la cumbre.

544   to climb

---

la clínica

545   clinic

---

recortar

546   to clip

---

el reloj

547   clock

---

cerrar

548   to close

---

el armario, el ropero

549   closet/cupboard*

---

la tela, el mantel, el paño

Las ropas se hacen con **tela.**
Hay **un mantel** en la mesa.
Mi mamá usa **un paño** de cocina para secar los platos.

Clothes are made out of cloth.
There is a tablecloth on the table.
Mother uses a dishcloth to wipe the dishes.

550   cloth

---

la ropa

551   clothes

---

el tendedero

552   clothes line

---

la nube

553   cloud

Los tréboles de cuatro hojas traen suerte.

554   clover

---

el payaso

555   clown

Cataplúm sale a cazar armado de **una maza**.

556   club

---

la pista, el indicio

La policía encontró **una pista** para resolver el delito.
Yo te voy a dar **un indicio**.

The police found a clue to the crime.
I will give you a clue.

557   clue

Los coches automáticos no tienen pedal de **embrague**.

558   clutch

¡**Agárrate** bien!

559   to clutch

Este es mi **entrenador**.

560   coach

Vamos viajando en **un bus** interprovincial.

561   coach

El carbón sale de las minas.

563   coal

tosco, grosero

Esta tela es muy **tosca**.
El es un tipo muy **grosero**.

This cloth is very coarse.
He is a very coarse man.

564   coarse

la costa, el litoral

565   coast

entrenar

Isabel **entrena** al equipo dos veces por semana.

Isabel coaches the team twice a week.

562   to coach

En invierno hace falta **un** buen **abrigo**.

566   coat

La casa de la araña se llama **telaraña**.

567   cobweb

el cacao

568   cocoa

el coco

569   coconut

el bacalao

570   cod

El **cafeto** es el árbol del **café**.

571   coffee

el ataúd

572   coffin

la espiral, el serpentín

573   coil

una moneda

574   coin

Tengo **frío**.

575   I am **cold**.

el cuello de la camisa

576   collar

La hermana de Lucía **colecciona** estampillas.

577   to **collect**

La universidad es una escuela para grandes.

578   college

Los coches **chocan** si se duermen los conductores.

579   to collide

un choque de automóviles

580   collision

¿Cuál es tu **color** preferido?

581   color/colours*

la yegua con su **potrillo**

582   colt

columnas de mármol

583   column

el peine, la peineta

584   comb

peinar

585   to comb

Combina bien los ingredientes.

586   combine

venir

Dile a Juan que **venga** a casa.
Marisol **vino** a la fiesta en autobús.
¿Tú **vienes** siempre por aquí?
¡**Vamos**, cuéntame!

Tell Juan to come home.
Marisol came to the party by bus.
Do you come here often?
Come on, tell me!

587   to come

Se me **soltó** en la mano.

588   to come off

Tuvo un desmayo, pero ya **volvió en sí.**

589   to come to

cómodo, confortable

590   comfortable

Una **coma** de verdad es mucho más pequeña.

591   comma

ordenar, mandar

592   to command

la comunidad, comunitario

Nosotros vivimos en **una comunidad** pequeña.
En el centro **comunitario** hay una piscina.
La construcción de la escuela fue un esfuerzo **comunitario.**

We live in a small community.
There is a pool at the community center.
Building the school was a community effort.

593   community

Martín y Daniel son **compañeros.**

594   companion

Estoy en buena **compañía.**

595   I am in good company.

comparar

596   to compare

Mi **brújula** apunta al norte.

597   My compass points north.

Ludwig **compone** una sinfonía.

el compositor

una **composición** para piano

el computador, la computadora, el ordenador

598   to compose

599   composer

600   composition

601   computer

concentrarse

el concierto

el concreto

el director de la orquesta

602   to concentrate

603   concert

604   concrete

605   conductor

el cono

el helado de **barquillo**

El fruto del pino se llama **piña**.

el conductor

607   cone

608   ice cream cone

609   pine cone

606   conductor/guard*

confiado

Estoy **confundido**.

felicitar, congratular

conectar

610   confident

611   I am confused.

612   to congratulate

613   to connect

la consonante

Las letras b, c, d, f, g son consonantes.

B, c, d, f, g are consonants.

Si te pierdes, pregúntale a **un policía**.

Una constelación tiene muchas estrellas.

En el mundo hay siete **continentes**.

614   consonant

615   constable

616   constellation

617   continent

una animada **conversación**

618 conversation

Mi papá es buen **cocinero**.

619 Dad is a good cook.

El **prepara** el desayuno.

620 He cooks breakfast.

¡No le robes **las galletas** a mamá!

621 cookie/biscuit*

Tengo la mano en agua **fría**.

622 My hand is in the **cool** water.

la cañería de **cobre**

623 copper

copiar

624 to **copy**

Este pececillo vive en un arrecife de **coral**.

625 coral

la cuerda, el cordel

626 cord

el corcho

627 cork

el sacacorchos, el tirabuzón

628 corkscrew

A Marisol le encanta comer **maíz**.

629 corn/maize*

el rincón

630 corner

el cadáver

631 corpse

el pasillo, el corredor

632 corridor

el cosmonauta

633 cosmonaut/astronaut*

un traje del siglo pasado

634 costume

la cabaña

635 cottage

la camisa de **algodón**

636 cotton

el sofá, el sillón

637 couch/sofa*

Manuela **tose** con discreción. **638** to **cough**	**contar** **639** to **count**
el contador **640** counter	¡Ponlo en **el mostrador**! **641** counter
¿Te gusta ir al **campo**? **642** country	Este **país** se llama Canadá. **643** country
Mi papá y mi mamá forman **una pareja**. **644** couple	Para pelear con dragones hace falta mucho **valor**. **645** courage
la cancha, **la pista** de tenis **646** court	Mi **prima** es la hija de mi tío. **647** My **cousin** is my uncle's daughter.
cubrir, tapar **648** to **cover**	Esta olla tiene **una tapa**. **649** cover
la vaca **650** cow	Este niño es un poco **cobarde**. **651** This boy is a **coward**.
el vaquero **652** cowboy	**Las jaibas** viven en el mar. **653** crab
Este florero tiene **una grieta**. **654** crack	**la galleta salada** **655** cracker
la cuna **656** cradle	**la garza, la grulla** **657** crane

la grúa

658   crane

estrellarse, chocar

659   to crash

¿Qué hay dentro de la caja?

660   crate

gatear

661   to crawl

el langostino

662   crayfish

los lápices de cera

663   crayons

la crema

A papá le gusta el café
con **crema**.
Me gustan los duraznos
con **crema**.
La crema para el sol te proteje
la piel.

*Dad likes cream in his coffee.
I like peaches and cream.
Sun cream protects your skin.*

664   cream

**la raya, el pliegue,
el doblez**

665   crease

¡Qué bicho más raro!

666   creature

**Un riachuelo es un río
pequeño.**

667   creek

la tripulación

668   the crew

la cuna

669   crib/cot*

el grillo

670   cricket

el criminal

671   criminal

el cocodrilo

672   crocodile

**Los azafranes brotan
en primavera.**

673   crocus

**¡Esa bribona robó
una manzana!**

674   crook

un palo torcido

675   crooked post

**El cuadro está torcido,
pero la torre está derecha.**

676   crooked painting, upright tower

una buena cosecha

677   crop

la cruz

678   cross

Mira bien antes de **cruzar**.

679   to cross

tachar, tarjar

680   to cross out

el cuervo

681   crow

un gentío muy grande en un espacio muy pequeño

682   A big **crowd** in a small space.

la corona

683   crown

Don Alfonso **corona** a la reina.

684   to crown

las migajas

685   crumb

Para hacer vino hay que **triturar** las uvas.

686   to crush

A Lucía le encanta **la corteza**.

687   crust

la muleta

688   crutch

llorar

689   to cry

la bola de **cristal**

690   crystal

Un osezno es un oso pequeño.

691   cub

el cubo

692   cube

el cuclillo

693   cuckoo

el pepino

694   cucumber

el puño de la camisa

695   cuff

la taza de té

696   cup

En **el aparador** hay un jarro.

697   cupboard

el borde de la acera, la cuneta 698　curb/kerb*	**curarse, sanar** 699　I am cured.	Adriana **se encrespó** el pelo. 700　to curl	Y ahora tiene el pelo **rizado**. 701　curly
Georgina es muy **curiosa**. 702　curious	**las grosellas** 703　currant	**la corriente** del río 704　current	**las cortinas** 705　curtains
la curva 706　curve	**el cojín** 707　cushion	**el cliente** 708　customer	**cortar** 709　to cut
linda, mona, graciosa 712　cute/sweet*	**la cuchillería, los cubiertos** 713　cutlery	**la bicicleta** 714　cycle	**ponerse por delante, interponerse** 710　to cut in
el cilindro 715　cylinder	**los platillos** 716　cymbals	**el ciprés** 717　cypress	¿Te gusta **recortar**? 711　to cut out

El narciso es una flor de primavera.

718 daffodil

el puñal

719 dagger

el diario, el periódico

720 daily

De las vacas obtenemos **productos lácteos**.

721 dairy

la margarita

722 daisy

Las represas están hechas de cemento.

723 dam

dañado, estropeado

724 damaged

húmedo

725 damp

bailar

726 to dance

la bailarina

727 dancer

El diente de león es una maleza.

728 dandelion

peligro

729 danger

¡Aquí está **oscuro**!

730 dark

¿Te gusta el juego de **los dardos**?

731 dart

el tablero de instrumentos

732 dashboard

¿Qué **fecha** es hoy?

733 date

Mi **hija** se llama Cristina.

734 daughter

Este va a ser un hermoso **día**.

735 the start of a nice day

un ratón **muerto**

736 dead mouse

No hay peor sordo que el que no quiere oír.

737 deaf

querido

Luis es un amigo muy **querido**.
¡**Querida m**amá, lo estoy pasando muy bien!
Mi hermano me es muy **querido**.

Luis is my dear friend.
Dear Mom, I'm having a great time!
My brother is very dear to me.

738 dear

Diciembre es el último mes del año.

739 December

decidir, decidirse

Marisol no logra **decidir** qué vestido ponerse.
Su mamá dice que tendrá que **decidirse** ahora mismo.

Marisol cannot decide what to wear.
Mom says she'll have to decide now.

740 to decide

la cubierta de un barco

741 deck

Este es el pirata Coqui **adornando** un arbolito.

742 to decorate

el adorno de Navidad

743 decoration

Rodrigo prefiere no nadar en la parte **profunda**.

744 deep end

Los venados viven en el bosque.

745 deer

entregar, repartir

746 to deliver

Martín me **abolló** el auto.

747 to dent

la dentista

748 dentist

las grandes tiendas, los grandes almacenes

749 department store

el desierto

750 desert

¿Qué hace **un escritorio** en el desierto?

751 desk

el postre

752 dessert

Godzilla **destruyó** toda la ciudad.

753 to destroy

Un destructor es un buque de guerra.

754 destroyer

un famoso **detective**

755 detective

Por la mañana hay **rocío** en las hojas.

756 dew

una línea **diagonal**

757　diagonal

el diagrama

758　diagram

el diamante

759　diamond

Los bebés necesitan **pañales**.

760　diaper/nappy*

Viviana lleva **un diario** de vida.

761　diary

Búscalo en **el diccionario**.

762　dictionary

morir, morirse

763　to die

la diferencia

Todas las personas nacen iguales; no hay ninguna **diferencia** entre ellas.
Hay mucha **diferencia** entre el día y la noche.

All people are born equal, there is no difference between them.
There is quite a difference between night and day.

764　difference

gentes **diferentes** . . . pero iguales

765　**different** people

cavar

766　to **dig**

La serpiente **digiere** un elefante.

767　The snake **digests** an elephant.

en **penumbras**

768　dim

A Lucía se le forman **hoyuelos** en las mejillas.

769　dimple

el bote de goma

770　dinghy

el comedor

771　dining room

la comida, la cena

772　dinner

el dinosaurio

773　dinosaur

la dirección, el rumbo

774　direction

Mi papá pisó donde había **mugre** . . .

775　dirt

. . . y se le pusieron los pantalones **sucios**.

776　dirty

Estoy en total **desacuerdo** contigo.
777 to disagree

La manzana de abajo **desapareció**.
778 to disappear

el desastre
779 disaster

descubrir
780 to discover

discutir
781 to discuss

la peste
782 disease

A Marisol le encantan **los disfraces.**
783 disguise

¡Marisol, ven a lavar **los platos**, por favor!
784 dishes

un tipo **deshonesto**
785 a dishonest person

agua de lavar los platos, lavazas
786 dishwater

¡No me gusta esta comida!
787 to dislike

La tableta **se disuelve** en el agua.
788 to dissolve

El espacio entre dos cosas se llama **distancia**.
789 distance between two trees

Decir **distante** es decir que está lejos.
790 a distant tree

Yo vivo en este **distrito**.
791 district

Estamos cavando **una zanja**.
792 ditch

zambullirse
793 to dive

Dividimos la manzana en dos.
794 to divide

Me siento **mareado**.
795 I feel dizzy.

¿Qué debo **hacer**?
796 What shall I do?

el muelle, el atracadero

797   dock

el doctor

798   doctor

¿Será éste **el perro** del hortelano?

799   dog

la muñeca

800   doll

el delfín

801   dolphin

la cúpula

802   dome

El burro de San Vicente lleva carga y no la siente.

803   donkey

la puerta

804   door

el tirador, el pomo, la perilla

805   doorknob

¿Ves **doble**?

806   double

Con **la masa** se hace el pan.

807   dough

La paloma es el símbolo de la paz.

808   dove

Marisol tiene una almohada de **plumón**.

809   down

dormitar

810   to doze

Una docena quiere decir doce.

811   dozen

¡No lo **arrastres** por el suelo!

812   to drag

el dragón

813   dragon

la libélula

814   dragonfly

el desagüe

815   drain/plug hole*

Martín **dibuja** muy bien.

816   to draw

¡Levanten **el puente levadizo**!

817 drawbridge

Marisol guarda su ropa en este **cajón**.

818 drawer

un hermoso **sueño**

819 a nice **dream**

Toti **sueña** con ovejitas.

820 I **dream** of sheep.

el vestido

821 dress

vestirse

822 to **dress**

El cajón de la ropa de Marisol es parte de esta **cómoda**.

823 **dresser/chest of drawers***

babear

824 to **dribble**

Quedar a la deriva no tiene ninguna gracia.

825 to **drift**

Gabriela **taladra** sobre la madera.

826 to **drill**

el taladro eléctrico

827 drill

el trago

828 drink

gotear

830 to **drip**

Yo **manejo** con mucho cuidado.

831 I **drive** carefully.

El conductor imprudente siempre termina mal.

832 crazy **driver**

tomar, beber

829 to **drink**

la llovizna

Hay una ligera **llovizna**.

There is a light drizzle.

833 drizzle

babear

834 to **drool**

No quedó ni **una gota**.

835 drop

Se me cayó la copa.

836 to **drop**

¡Te **vine a ver** de paso!

837   to **drop** in

Papá **pasó a dejar** el gato al veterinario.

838   Dad **drops off** the cat at the vet.

abandonar, salirse

839   to **drop** out

Me siento muy **amodorrado**.

840   I feel **drowsy**.

el tambor

841   drum

seco

842   dry

secar

843   to **dry**

limpiado **en seco**

844   dry cleaner

Pon la ropa mojada en **la secadora**.

845   dryer

la duquesa

846   duchess

el pato

847   duck

Batirse a duelo no soluciona nada.

848   duel

el duque

849   duke

el basural, el vertedero, el basurero

850   dump

botar, descargar

851   to **dump**

el camión de volteo, el camión tolva

852   dumptruck/lorry*

El ladrón lleva años en **el calabozo**.

853   dungeon

el crepúsculo

854   dusk

el polvo

855   dust

el enano

856   dwarf

E

Cada uno tiene una zanahoria.

857 **Each** rabbit has a carrot.

Las águilas son aves en peligro de extinción.

858 eagle

el oído, la oreja

859 ear

No por mucho madrugar amanece más **temprano**.

860 early

ganar, ganarse

Mi mamá **gana** un buen sueldo.
Marisol se ha **ganado**
unas vacaciones. ,
El dinero tienes que **ganártelo**
antes de poder gastarlo.

Mom earns a good wage.
Marisol has earned a holiday.
You must earn it before you
spend it.

861 to **earn**

el planeta Tierra

862 Earth

la palada de **tierra**

863 earth

el terremoto

864 earthquake

el caballete, el atril

865 easel

El este es lo mismo que el oriente.

866 east

Aprender a nadar es muy **fácil**.

867 Swimming is **easy**.

comer

868 to **eat**

tomar el desayuno

869 to **eat breakfast**

almorzar

870 to **eat lunch**

comer, cenar

871 to **eat dinner/supper***

¿Oyes **el eco** . . . eco . . . eco . . .?

872 echo

el eclipse de sol

873 eclipse

El árbol está al **borde** del barranco

874 The tree is at the **edge**.

la anguila

875 eel

La gallina francolina puso **un huevo** en la cocina. 876 egg	**la berenjena** 877 eggplant/aubergine*	**ocho** 878 eight	**octavo** 879 eighth
el elástico 880 elastic	**el codo** 881 elbow	**la elección** Los gobiernos se eligen por medio de **las elecciones**. ¿Quién ganó **las elecciones**? Esta **elección** fue muy reñida. *Elections are held to choose the government.* *Who won the election?* *The election was very close.* 882 election	**el electricista** 883 electrician
la electricidad 884 electricity	**el elefante** 885 elephant	**el ascensor** 886 elevator/lift*	**el ante** 887 elk
el olmo 888 elm	Mario me **dejó en vergüenza**. 889 to embarrass	**abrazar, abrazarse** 890 to embrace	**el bordado** 891 embroidery
la emergencia 892 emergency	Este frasco está **vacío**. 893 The jar is **empty**.	Este es **el fin** del camino. 894 This is the **end**.	Ojalá que algún día dejen de ser **enemigos**. 895 enemies

el motor de un coche

896   engine

el maquinista

897   engineer/engine driver*

saborear, disfrutar, gozar

898   to enjoy

un dinosaurio **enorme**

899   **enormous** dinosaur

Con eso **basta**.

900   That is **enough**.

entrar

901   to enter

la entrada

902   entrance

el sobre

903   envelope

iguales

904   equal

el ecuador

905   equator

el mandado, la diligencia

Marisol salió a hacer **un mandado** para su papá.
Tiene muchas **diligencias** que hacer esta mañana.

Marisol is running an errand for Dad.
She has many errands this morning.

906   errand

Una escalera mecánica sube y la otra baja.

907   escalator

Consiguió **escaparse**.

908   to escape

Europa es un continente.

909   Europe

la evaporación

910   evaporation

El cuatro es número **par**.

$n \times 2 = ?$

911   Four is an **even** number.

una superficia **pareja**

912   an **even** surface

el siempre verde

913   evergreen

todo, cada

Marisol hace la cama casi **todos** los días.
¿Cómo es posible que su mamá se lo tenga que decir **cada** vez?

Marisol makes her bed almost every day.
Must Mom tell her every time?

914   every

Algunos **exámenes** son fáciles, otros no.

915   exam

examinar

916   to examine

el ejemplo

A veces Marisol no da muy buen **ejemplo**.
Las cosas se entienden más fácilmente cuando se pone **un ejemplo**.

Sometimes Marisol does not set a good example.
Things are easier to understand when you give an example.

917   example

el signo de exclamación

918   exclamation mark

¡Disculpe!

919   Excuse me!

María Paz **hace ejercicios** todos los días.

920   to exercise

existir

Existir es lo mismo que ser.
Marisol dice "no hay tal cosa" cuando quiere decir "eso no **existe**".

To exist is to be.
Marisol said "There is no such thing", and she meant "It does not exist".

921   to exist

salir

922   to exit/leave*

Este globo se va a **expandir** hasta reventarse.

923   to expand

esperar, contar con

Te **esperamos** a las dos de la tarde.
Papá **cuenta con** que te portes bien.
Anita no puede **esperar** otra cosa.

We expect you at two o'clock.
Dad expects you to be good.
Anita cannot expect any more.

924   to expect

caro

925   expensive

el experimento

926   experiment

la experta

927   expert

Déjame **explicarte** lo que pasa.

928   to explain

explorar

929   to explore

la explosión

930   explosion

el extintor de incendios

931   extinguisher

el ojo

932   eye

la ceja

933   eyebrow

los anteojos, los lentes, las gafas

934   eyeglasses/spectacles*

la pestaña

935   eyelash

936 fable — ¿Conoces **la fábula** de la hormiga y el saltamontes?

937 face — la cara, el rostro

938 factory — la fábrica

939 to fail — Juan **reprobó** el examen.

940 to fail — fallar, averiarse

941 fair — la feria

942 fairy — ¿Te gustan los cuentos de **hadas**?

943 faith — la fe

Tenemos mucha **fe** en ti. Marisol aceptó de buena **fe**.

We have faith in you. Marisol accepted it in good faith.

944 fake painting — Este cuadro es **falso**.

945 fall/autumn* — En **el otoño** se caen las hojas.

946 to fall — caer, caerse

949 false alarm — ¡Una **falsa** alarma! Era un asado a la parrilla.

950 family — la familia

947 to fall down — caer, caerse al suelo

948 to fall off — caerse de

951 famous actress — Maricarmen es una actriz muy **famosa**.

952 fan — el ventilador

953 fancy clothes — trajes **elegantes, de fantasía**

954 fang — el colmillo

La ciudad está **lejos**.
955 The city is **far** away.

¡**Que te vaya bien!**
956 Farewell !

En **las granjas** se cultiva la tierra.
957 farm

el granjero
958 farmer

rápido, veloz
959 fast

Yo siempre **me abrocho** el cinturón de seguridad.
960 I **fasten** my seatbelt.

Al **gordo** Hernán le gustan los dulces.
961 fat

Ingerir substancias venenosas es **mortal**.
962 fatal

el padre
963 father

Esta **llave** gotea.
964 faucet/tap*

Los dos se echan **la culpa**.
965 Whose **fault** is it?

el favor
¿Te puedo pedir **un favor**? Marisol es buena persona y le gusta hacer **favores**.

Can I ask you a favor? Marisol is nice and likes doing people favors.
966 favor/favour*

mi helado **favorito**
967 favorite/favourite*

¿Quién le **tiene miedo** al lobo?
968 to **fear** the worst

el festín
969 feast

Antiguamente **las plumas** se usaban para escribir.
970 feather

Febrero es el segundo mes del año.
971 February

Juanita **alimenta** al bebé cada cuatro horas.
972 to feed

Me siento muy bien.
973 I **feel** well.

La hembra es la que pone los huevos.
974 female

la cerca, la reja, la valla, la verja 975 fence	**el guardafango, el tapabarro** 976 fender/wing*	**el helecho** 977 fern	**el transbordador** 978 ferry
el festival 979 festival	Pobre Jorge, tiene mucha **fiebre**. 980 fever	Vino **poca** gente. 981 Few people came.	**un campo** 982 field
Eliana es la **quinta** del grupo. 983 fifth	Estos dos se llevan mal y no hacen más que **pelear**. 984 to fight	**limar, limarse** 985 to file	**llenar** 986 to fill
un rollo de **película** 988 film	Este cerdo **inmundo** no se baña jamás. 989 filthy	**la aleta** de tiburón 990 fin	**llenar** 987 to fill up
una **multa** por exceso de velocidad 991 fine	Estoy **bien**. 992 I am fine.	**el dedo** 993 finger	**las huellas digitales, las huellas dactilares** 994 fingerprint

terminar

995   to finish

De **los abetos** se saca la trementina.

996   fir

el fuego, el incendio

997   fire

el camión de bomberos, la bomba, el carrobomba

998   fire engine

la escalera de incendio

999   fire escape

el petardo

1000   firecracker/banger*

el bombero

1001   firefighter

la chimenea, el hogar

1002   fireplace

firme, la firma

Marisol me dio un **firme** apretón de manos.
La firma de Lucía fabrica juguetes.
El abuelo se puso **firme** y no quiere que Martín tome otro helado más.

Marisol gave me a firm handshake.
Lucia's firm makes toys.
Grandpa's decision is firm, Martin cannot have another ice cream.

1003   firm

el primero de la fila

1004   first

Los pescados vivos se llaman **peces**.

1005   fish

pescar

1006   to fish

el anzuelo

1007   fishhook

el puño

1008   fist

el número cinco

1009   five

¿Crees tú que lo puede **arreglar**?

1010   to fix

la bandera pirata

1011   flag

los copos de nieve

1012   flake

la llama

1013   flame

¿Por qué **aleteas** tanto, pajarito?

1014   to flap

Las luces de bengala sirven para hacer señales.	**el fogonazo**	**la linterna**	**el frasco**
1015 flare	1016 flash	1017 flashlight/torch*	1018 flask
plano, liso	El uslero sirve para **aplanar** la masa.	¿Qué **sabor** te gusta más?	Capitán tiene **una pulga** en el lomo.
1019 flat	1020 to flatten	1021 flavor/flavour*	1022 flea
Roberto **huyó** al ver al marciano.	**el vellón**	Este caballero es bastante entrado en **carnes**.	**flotar**
1023 to flee	1024 fleece	1025 flesh	1026 to float
la bandada de pájaros	**la inundación**	**el suelo, el piso**	De **la harina** sale el pan.
1027 flock	1028 flood	1029 floor	1030 flour
La sangre **corre** hacia la vena.	**la flor**	Luis está en cama con **influenza**.	**la pelusa**
1031 to flow	1032 flower	1033 flu	1034 fluff

El agua es **un fluido**.

1035　　fluid

la mosca

1036　　fly

¡Súbete **el cierre**!

1037　　fly

Los pájaros y los aviones pueden **volar**.

1038　　to fly

la espuma

1039　　foam

La neblina no me deja ver.

1040　　fog

Dóblalo para este lado.

1041　　to fold

El ganso **sigue** a Martín a todas partes.

1042　　to follow

la comida, el alimento

1043　　food

el pie

1044　　foot

la pelota, el balón

1045　　American football

una pisada sobre la nieve

1046　　footprint

Oigo unos **pasos** detrás de mí.

1047　　footsteps

para, por

Todos **para** uno y uno **para** todos.
De una vez **por** todas.
Si no fuera **por** ti, habríamos perdido el partido.

One for all and all for one.
Once and for all.
But for you, we would have lost the game.

1048　　for

forzar

1049　　to force

la frente

1050　　forehead

En **el bosque** viven muchos animalitos.

1051　　forest

olvidar, olvidarse

A mi perro se le **olvida** su nombre.
Papá **olvidó** comprar la leche.
¡**Olvídalo**!

Our dog forgets his name.
Dad forgot to buy milk.
Forget it!

1052　　to forget

perdonar

Te **perdono** si prometes portarte bien.
Marisol **perdonó** a su perro por comerle una muñeca.

I forgive you if you promise to be good.
Marisol forgave her dog for eating her favorite doll.

1053　　to forgive

el tenedor

1054　　fork

la grúa de horquilla

1055   forklift

el maniquí

1056   form/tailor's dummy*

A cargo del **fuerte** está la guarnición.

1057   fort

adelante, atrevido, avanzado

¿Quién quiere salir **adelante**?
Marisol opina que el tipo es muy **atrevido**.
Las tropas están en posición **avanzada**.

*Who would like to come forward?
Marisol thinks he is
too forward.
The troops are in a forward
position.*

1058   forward

Los restos **fósiles** de un pescado.

1059   fossil

un olor **fétido**

1060   foul odor/odour*

los cimientos de una casa

1061   foundation

la fuente

1062   fountain

Los zorros son muy astutos.

1063   fox

una fracción del pastel

1064   fraction

Los huevos son muy **frágiles**.

1065   fragile

el marco

1066   frame

pocas **pecas**

1067   freckle

libre

1068   free

A Inuk se le **congeló** el refresco.

1069   to freeze

una manzana **fresca**, recién cortada

1070   fresh

el viernes

El amigo de Róbinson Crusoe se llamaba igual que el día **viernes**.

Robinson Crusoe's friend was named after this day.

1071   Friday

Algunos lo llaman **refrigerador**, otros **nevera**.

1072   fridge

las amigas

1073   friends

A María le encanta **asustar** a su hermano.

1074   to frighten

La rana es un batracio.

1075　　frog

Yo vengo **del** planeta Marte.

1076　　I am **from** Mars.

la parte de adelante

1077　　front

¿Ves **la escarcha** en la ventana?

1078　　frost

¿Por qué **frunces el ceño**?

1079　　to **frown**

La fruta es mucho mejor que los caramelos.

1080　　fruit

freír

1081　　to **fry**

la sartén

1082　　frying pan

Los autos funcionan con **combustible**.

1083　　Cars need **fuel**.

lleno, colmado

1084　　full

diversión, entretenimiento

1085　　having **fun**

un fondo de ayuda para las personas necesitadas

1086　　charity **fund**

Cuando muere alguien se hace **un funeral**.

1087　　funeral

¿Conoces la ley del **embudo**?

1088　　funnel

gracioso, divertido, raro

Ese es un payaso muy **gracioso**.
Me pasó algo muy **divertido** camino de la escuela.
Marisol se sintió muy **rara** después de comer champiñones.

That's a very funny clown.
A funny thing happened on the way to school.
Marisol felt funny after eating that mushroom.

1089　　funny

¿Un abrigo de **pieles** en pleno verano?

1090　　fur coat

Mi casa se calienta con **una caldera**.

1091　　furnace/boiler*

los muebles

1092　　furniture

¿Se quemaron **los fusibles**?

1094　　fuse

Micifuz es un gatito muy **lanudo**.

1093　　furry

G

Un ventarrón es un viento muy fuerte.

1095   gale

la galería de arte

1096   gallery

Los caballos caminan, trotan y **galopan**.

1097   to gallop

A Pablo le encantan **los juegos**.

1098   game

El ganso es macho, la gansa es hembra.

1099   gander

la pandilla de ladrones

1100   gang

Marisol tiene **un hueco** entre los dientes.

1101   gap

El auto está guardado en **la cochera**.

1102   garage

la basura

1103   garbage/rubbish*

el cubo, el tacho o tarro de la basura

1104   garbage can/rubbish bin*

la huerta, el jardín

1105   vegetable **garden**

hacer gárgaras

1106   to gargle

El ajo tiene un sabor muy fuerte.

1107   garlic

Las ligas sirven para afirmar las medias.

1108   garter

el gas

Algunos globos se inflan con **gas**.
Hay **gases** que son más livianos que el aire.
Los bomberos usan máscara de **gas** para protegerse del humo.

The balloon was filled with gas.
Some gases are lighter than air.
Firemen wear gas masks against the smoke.

1109   gas

Algunos la llaman **gasolina**, otros **bencina**.

1110   gas/petrol*

El pedal de la bencina se llama **acelerador**.

1111   gas pedal/accelerator*

la bomba de gasolina

1112   gas/petrol pump*

la gasolinera, la estación de servicio

1113   gas/petrol station*

la puerta, el portón

1114   gate

Esta señora está **recogiendo** flores.

1115   to **gather**

los engranajes

1116   gears

la piedra preciosa, la gema

1117   gem

Los generales están muy generalizados.

1118   general

un amigo **generoso**

1119   a **generous** friend

una persona **bondadosa**

1120   a **gentle** person

Mi papá es todo un **caballero**.

1121   gentleman

un cerdo **legítimo**

1122   a **genuine** pig

En las escuelas se estudia **la geografía**.

1123   geography

el geranio

1124   geranium

Los gerbos son unos roedores muy simpáticos.

1125   gerbil

Los gérmenes causan muchas enfermedades.

1126   germ

¡Micifuz, **agarra** ese ratón!

1127   **Get** that mouse!

Quiero que me **devuelvas** mi libro.

1128   I want to **get** it **back**.

Marisol **se mete** despacito.

1129   to **get in** the pool

Marisol **se baja** . . .

1130   to **get off**

. . . y **se sube**.

1131   to **get on**

Sale a **botar** la basura . . .

1132   to **get rid of**

. . . pero primero **se levanta**.

1133   to **get up**

¿Le tienes miedo a **los fantasmas**?

1134   ghost

el gigante

1135   giant

el regalo, el obsequio

1136   gift

una ballena **gigantesca**

1137   gigantic

reírse tontamente

1138   to giggle

Los peces tienen muchas **agallas**.

1139   gills

El jengibre se usa para cocinar.

1140   ginger

una figurita de **pan de jengibre**

1141   gingerbread

Los gitanos siempre viajan en caravanas.

1142   gipsy

¿Sabes por qué **las jirafas** no usan corbata?

1143   giraffe

la niña

1144   girl

Yo le **di** mi paraguas porque ella no tenía.

1145   to give

el glaciar

1148   glacier

Me **alegro**.

1149   I am glad.

Las ventanas se hacen de **vidrio**.

1150   glass

Cuando escampó, ella me lo **devolvió**.

1146   to give back

¿Tú usas **anteojos**?

1152   glasses

deslizarse

1153   to glide

el vaso de agua

1151   glass

¡Me **rindo**!

1147   I give up!

el planeador

1154　　glider

los guantes

1155　　gloves

La goma sirve para pegar.

1156　　glue

ir

1157　　to **go**

El arquero defiende **el arco**.

1161　　goal

Algunas **cabras** son domésticas, otras no.

1162　　goat

Los lentes protectores se usan para nadar.

1163　　goggles

El técnico **baja** a hacer su trabajo.

1158　　to **go** down

la barra de **oro**

1164　　gold

Yo me río de **los peces de colores**.

1165　　goldfish

El Tío Lalo es muy bueno para **el golf**.

1166　　golf

Capitán **entró** a dormir una siesta.

1159　　to **go** in

una **buena** comida

1167　　good

¡Adiós, mamá!

1168　　Goodbye!

la gansa

1169　　goose

Juanito **subió** por la mata de frijoles.

1160　　to **go** up

la grosella silvestre

1170　　gooseberry

Esta señora se cree **muy hermosa**.

1171　　gorgeous

el gorila

1172　　gorilla

gobernar

El gobierno **gobierna** el país.
Gobernar un país no es tan fácil como parece.

The government governs the country.
It is not as easy to govern a country as it seems.

1173　　to **govern**

el gobierno

Al **gobierno** lo elige el pueblo.
El papá de Marisol es un almirante y trabaja para **el gobierno.**

The government is elected by the people.
Marisol's dad, the admiral, works for the government.

1174   government

arrebatar

1175   to grab

Él es muy gentil.

1176   He is very gracious.

Estoy en primer grado.

1177   grade / form*

El grano cosechado se guarda en los graneros.

1178   grain

1000 **gramos** = 1 kilo

1179   gram

el nieto, la nieta

1180   grandchild

el abuelo

1181   grandfather

A **la abuela** de Marisol le gusta tocar la batería.

1182   grandmother

El granito es una piedra muy dura.

1183   granite

otorgar, conceder

Le voy a **otorgar** diez días de licencia.
Tu hada madrina te va a **conceder** tres deseos.

I grant you ten days' leave of absence.
The good fairy will grant you three wishes.

1184   to grant

un racimo de **uvas**

1185   grapes

la toronja, el pomelo

1186   grapefruit

el gráfico

1187   graph

el césped, el pasto, la hierba

1188   grass

el saltamontes

1189   grasshopper

el rallador

1190   grater

la tumba, la sepultura

1191   grave

Siempre hay **ripio** a la orilla del camino.

1192   gravel

La fuerza de **gravedad** hace que la manzana caiga.

1193   Gravity makes apples fall.

Las vaquitas salieron a **pastar.**
1194   to **graze**

Con un poco de **grasa** se acaban los ruidos.
1195   **grease**

un **magnífico** juguete
1196   a **great** toy

avaricioso, codicioso
1197   **greedy**

Verde, que te quiero **verde** . . .
1198   **green**

los porotos, los frijoles, las habichuelas, las judías
1199   **green** bean

el **invernadero**
1200   **greenhouse**

Martín siempre **saluda** a las damas.
1201   to **greet**

el **gris**
1202   **grey*/gray**

asar a la parrilla
1203   to **grill**

mugriento
1204   **grimy**

Jesús **sonríe** porque está contento.
1205   to **grin**

Mamá **muele** carne para la comida.
1206   to **grind**/to **mince***

Agárrate del manubrio con fuerza.
1207   to **grip**

quejarse
1208   to **groan**

El almacenero de mi barrio es buena persona.
1209   **grocer**

En la tienda de **abarrotes** se compran **los comestibles.**
1210   shopping for **groceries**

la novia y **el novio**
1211   **groom**

el **mozo de cuadra,** el **palafrenero**
1212   **groom**

Gabriela **se acicala** frente al espejo.
1213   to **groom**

la acanaladura, la estría, la ranura, el surco

1214   groove

¡Qué monstruo más repugnante!

1215   gross/disgusting*

el suelo, la tierra

1216   ground

la marmota

1217   groundhog

el grupo de gente

1218   group

¿Ves cómo **crece** la planta?

1219   to grow

gruñir

1220   to growl

una persona mayor

1221   grown-up

montar guardia, vigilar

1222   to guard

adivina, buen adivinador . . .

1223   to guess

Igor le abrió la puerta al **huésped** . . .

1224   guest

. . . y lo **condujo** a su habitación.

1225   to guide

culpable

Marisol dice que no es **culpable.**
¿Quién es **culpable** de este robo?
El ladrón se declaró **culpable.**

Marisol says she is not guilty.
Who is guilty of this theft?
The thief pleaded guilty.

1226   guilty

Los conejillos de Indias comen a la carta.

1227   guinea pig

la guitarra

1228   guitar

el Golfo de México

1229   Gulf of Mexico

Las gaviotas viven cerca del agua.

1230   gull

Encías sanas, dientes sanos.

1231   gum

Mascar **chicle** es pésima costumbre.

1232   gum/chewing gum*

El agua corre por **la cuneta.**

1233   gutter

H

una mala **costumbre**

1234 bad **habit**

El abadejo es un tipo de bacalao.

1235 haddock

una tempestad de **granizo**

1236 hail

La hermana de Marisol tiene **una cabellera** abundante.

1237 hair

el cepillo para el pelo

1238 hairbrush

el peluquero, el peinador

1239 hairdresser

Este **secador de pelo** parece casco de astronauta.

1240 hairdryer

¿Quieres **la mitad?**

1241 half

el vestíbulo

1242 hall

La noche de **Halloween** las brujas hacen un aquelarre.

1243 Halloween/Hallowe'en*

el pasillo

1244 hallway/corridor*

Al llegar a la garita nos **detuvo** un guardia.

1245 to halt

el martillo

1246 hammer

Gonzalo **martillea** de lo lindo.

1247 to hammer

la hamaca

1248 hammock

El hámster es chico y abunda en Europa.

1249 hamster

la mano

1250 hand

repartir, distribuir

1251 to hand out

el freno de mano

1252 hand brake

Estas **esposas** no se casan con nadie.

1253 handcuffs

el impedimento, el obstáculo

La ceguera es **un impedimento**.
Pero las personas pueden vencer cualquier **obstáculo**.

Being blind is a handicap. People can overcome any handicap.

1254 handicap

la manija, la manilla

1255 handle

el pasamanos, la baranda

1256 handrail

apuesto, guapo, bien parecido

1257 handsome

un tipo **diestro, hábil**

1258 handy person

¡**Cuelga** bien el cuadro!

1259 to hang

aferrarse, agarrarse

1260 to hang on

el hangar

1262 hangar

Cuelga tu abrigo en este **colgador**.

1263 hanger

el pañuelo

1264 handkerchief

colgar

1261 to hang up

A todos nos puede **pasar** un accidente.

1265 Accidents **happen**.

Silvio está **contento**, pero su hermana no.

1266 He is **happy**.

Los buques están anclados en **el puerto**.

1267 harbor/harbour*

No lc puedo romper, está muy **duro**.

1268 hard

la liebre

1269 hare

¡Nunca le **hagas daño** a un animalito!

1270 to harm

la armónica

1271 harmonica

Los caballos usan **un arnés**.

1272 harness

el arpa
1273   harp

El invierno pasado fue muy **crudo**.
1274   a **harsh** winter

Don Segundo **cosechando** el trigo.
1275   to **harvest**

el sombrero
1276   hat

Los pollitos **empollan** en 21 días.
1277   to **hatch**

la hachuela
1278   hatchet

Luis el filibustero **acarreando** el botín.
1279   to **haul**

una casa **embrujada, encantada**
1280   **haunted** house

A Pepita le gustaría **tener** la misma muñeca.
1281   to **have**

el halcón
1282   hawk

heno para los caballos
1283   hay

Los días de **bruma** no se puede ver bien.
1284   **Haze** makes for a hazy day.

el avellano
1285   hazel

la avellana
1286   hazelnut

la cabeza
1287   head

Tengo un terrible **dolor de cabeza**.
1288   I have a **headache**.

la cabecera, el reposacabeza
1289   headrest

La pierna rota ya está **sanando**.
1290   to **heal**

Una flor **lozana**, otra marchita.
1291   **healthy** flower

un montón de basura
1292   heap/pile*

Oigo una voz.

1293   I **hear** a voice.

el corazón

1294   heart

calentar

1295   to **heat**

el calefactor, el aparato de calefacción

1296   heater/radiator*

levantar, alzar en vilo

1297   to **heave**

el cielo

1298   heaven

un elefante **pesado**

1299   one **heavy** elephant

¿Quién sabe podar **el seto**?

1300   hedge

Un erizo no es lo mismo que un puercoespín.

1301   hedgehog

el talón

1302   heel

el helicóptero

1303   helicopter

el infierno

1304   hell

¡Hola!

1305   hello

El rumbo se cambia con un golpe de **timón**.

1306   helm

Los soldados usan **cascos**.

1307   helmet

A la mamá de Marisol también le gusta **ayudar**.

1308   to **help**

Los recién nacidos son **indefensos**.

1309   helpless

la bastilla, el ruedo

1310   hem

el hemisferio

1311   hemisphere

la gallina

1312   hen

Un heptágono
tiene siete lados.

1313   heptagon

las hierbas o yerbas

1314   herbs

un rebaño de vacas

1315   herd

¡Ven aquí!

1316   Come here!

Los ermitaños
no tienen teléfono.

1317   hermit

el héroe

1318   hero

la heroína

1319   heroine

el arenque

1320   herring

Jorge **titubea**
antes de zambullirse.

1321   to hesitate

Un hexágono
tiene seis lados.

1322   hexagon

Los osos **hibernan**
todo el invierno.

1323   to hibernate

tener hipo, hipar

1324   to hiccup/hiccough*

El cuero de un animal es
lo mismo que tu piel.

1325   hide

esconderse

1326   to hide

el escondite

1327   hiding-place

una montaña muy **alta**

1328   a high mountain

un edificio
de varios pisos

1329   highrise/tower block*

el liceo,
la escuela secundaria

1330   high school/secondary school*

la carretera,
la autopista

1331   highway/motorway*

Secuestrar un avión es
muy feo.

1332   to hijack a plane

Sobre **la colina** hay un arbolito.

1333 hill

la bisagra, el gozne

1334 hinge

las patas traseras

1335 hind legs

mano en **cadera**

1336 hand on hip

A **los hipopótamos** no les da hipo.

1337 hippopotamus

Yo estudio **historia**.

1338 I study **history**.

Para clavar bien tienes que **golpear** con fuerza.

1339 to hit

Las abejas viven en **colmenas**.

1340 hive

acaparar

1341 to **hoard**

Hoy grité hasta quedar **ronco**.

1342 **hoarse** voice

Tejer es **el pasatiempo** de mamá.

1343 hobby

Mi hermano es jugador de **hockey**.

1344 hockey/ice hockey*

la azada, el azadón

1347 hoe

Marisol **sostiene** en el aire a Micifuz.

1348 to **hold**

Pero no está bien **sujetarlo** de esa forma.

1349 to **hold down**

el tejo de hockey

1345 hockey puck

el agujero, el hoyo

1350 hole

Orlando se merece unas **vacaciones**.

1351 holiday

Las ardillas viven en troncos **huecos**.

1352 **hollow** tree

el bastón de hockey

1346 hockey stick

El acebo se usa como adorno de Navidad.

1353   holly

En la India las vacas son **sagradas**.

1354   a **holy** cow

Las ardillas están **en casa**.

1355   **home**

las tareas, los deberes

1356   **homework**

¿Será un tipo **honrado**?

1357   Is he **honest**?

A los osos les encanta **la miel**.

1358   **honey**

el panal

1359   **honeycomb**

el melón

1360   **honeydew** melon

tocar la bocina

1361   to **honk**

graduado con **distinción**

1362   **honor/honour***

El abrigo de Marisol tiene **una capucha**.

1363   **hood**

Para ver el motor hay que levantar **el capó**.

1364   **hood/bonnet***

Los caballos tienen **cascos**.

1365   **hoof**

el anzuelo

1366   **hook**

¡Salta por **el aro**!

1367   jump through a **hoop**

brincar

1368   to **hop**

Espero ganar.

1369   I **hope** to win.

un mal jinete **sin remedio**

1370   **hopeless**

la rayuela, la reina mora, la pata coja, el luche, el piso

1371   **hopscotch/hop-scotch***

El sol se levanta en **el horizonte**.

1372   **horizon**

horizontal
1373 horizontal

la bocina
1374 horn

el corno francés
1375 French **horn**

el cuerno
1376 horn

Las avispas pican muy fuerte.
1377 hornet

el caballo
1378 horse

¿Te gustan **los rábanos picantes**?
1379 horseradish

La herradura da suerte.
1380 horseshoe

la manguera
1381 hose

el hospital
1382 hospital

Un día muy **caluroso**.
1383 hot

Los niños no deben comer cosas muy **picantes**.
1384 hot

Los hoteles dan alojamiento a los viajeros.
1386 hotel

Una hora tiene sesenta minutos.
1387 hour

el reloj de arena
1388 hourglass

Para comer **ají** hay que tener mucho cuidado.
1385 hot pepper

la casa
1389 house

el aerodeslizador
1390 hovercraft

Déjame mostrarte **cómo** se hace.
1391 I will show you **how.**

aullar
1392 to howl

el tapacubos
1393   hub cap

el arándano
1394   huckleberry

apiñarse, amontonarse
1395   to huddle

enorme
1396   huge

el casco
1397   hull

el colibrí, el picaflor
1398   hummingbird

la joroba, la giba
1399   hump

cien, ciento
1400   hundred

Tiene mucha **hambre.**
1401   She is **hungry.**

cazar
1402   to hunt

lanzar, arrojar
1403   to hurl

¿Quién será el que bautiza a **los huracanes**?
1404   hurricane

apresurarse, apurarse, darse prisa
1405   to hurry

Me **duele** la muñeca.
1406   My wrist **hurts.**

Este es mi **marido.**
1407   husband

la choza
1408   hut

el aparador, la alacena
1409   hutch/sideboard*

el jacinto
1410   hyacinth

El coro cantó **el himno** nacional.
1411   hymn

el guión

El guión sirve para separar palabras compuestas.

Hyphens are short lines between words that belong together.

1412   hyphen

Dos cubos de **hielo** en un vaso.

1413   ice

el helado

1414   ice cream

Los témpanos de hielo son un peligro para la navegación.

1415   iceberg

el carámbano

1416   icicle

el decorado de una torta

1417   icing

¡Se me acaba de ocurrir **una idea**!

1418   idea

Los gemelos son **idénticos.**

1419   identical twins

el idiota

1420   idiot

ocioso, inactivo

1421   idle

si

Si tuviera un martillo, clavaría donde no molestara a nadie.
Te lo compraría si pudiera.

If I had a hammer, I would only hammer when no one is sleeping.
I would buy it for you if I could.

1422   if

el iglú

1423   igloo

la llave de encendido o contacto

1424   ignition key

Jorge lleva varios días **enfermo.**

1425   ill

iluminar, alumbrar

1426   to illuminate

la ilustración

Las imágenes de un libro se llaman **ilustraciones**.
Este diccionario tiene muchas **ilustraciones**.

Pictures in a book are called illustrations.
This dictionary has many illustrations.

1427   illustration

importante

Este es un asunto muy **importante.**
Lo que es **importante** para Marisol quizás no sea **importante** para Martín.

This is an important matter.
What is important to Marisol may not be important to Martin.

1428   important

en, de

Pancho está en el hospital.
Esta sala tiene cuatro metros, **de** largo.
Marisol está vestida **de** blanco.

Pancho is in hospital.
This room is four metres in length.
Marisol is dressed in white.

1429   in

El incienso se quema en un incensario.

1430   incense

Doce **pulgadas** equivalen a un pie.

1431   inch

el índice

Al final de este libro encontrarás **un índice**. Ese **índice** contiene todas las palabras que aparecen en este diccionario.

There is an index at the back of the book.
The index contains all the words in this dictionary.

1432　　index

el añil, el índigo

1433　　indigo

dentro de la casa

1434　　indoors

la criatura

1435　　infant

Tía Tita se pescó **una infección.**

1436　　infection

infeccioso, contagioso

Su estado es **infeccioso**.
Cualquiera puede agarrar una enfermedad **infecciosa**.
Papá tiene una risa **contagiosa**.

Her condition is infectious.
You could catch an infectious disease.
Dad has an infectious laugh.

1437　　infectious

Delatar a alguien es indigno.

1438　　to inform

Este oso **habita** en una cueva.

1439　　The bear **inhabits** a cave.

¿Cuáles son tus **iniciales?**

1440　　initials

El doctor me puso **una inyección**.

1441　　injection

la herida

1442　　injury

la tinta

1443　　ink

Existen muchos tipos de **insectos**.

1444　　insect

Este niño está **dentro** de la caja.

1445　　inside

Perdona que **insista,** pero . . .

1446　　to insist

inspeccionar

1447　　to inspect

Usa una cuchara **en lugar de** un tenedor.

1449　　Use a spoon **instead** of a fork!

la enseñanza

1450　　instruction

el instructor, el profesor, el maestro

1451　　instructor

el inspector

1448　　inspector

**el aislante,
el aislamiento**

Las murallas de mi casa tienen **aislante** para que no entre el frío.
Los cables eléctricos tienen **aislamiento** para que no nos dé la corriente.

There is insulation in the walls of the house.
There is insulation around the wires so people will not get a shock.

1452　insulation

la intersección, el cruce

1453　intersection/crossroads*

la entrevista

1454　interview

Domingo entró **a** su cuarto.

1455　**into** the room

Liliana me **presentó** a sus amigos.

1456　to introduce

Los vikingos **invadieron** muchos países.

1457　to invade

Con tanta guerra, algunos quedaron **inválidos**.

1458　invalid

¿Quién habrá **inventado** los árboles?

1459　to invent

¿Has visto al hombre **invisible**?

1460　invisible

Alguien me trajo **una invitación**.

1461　invitation

El que **invita** es él.

1462　He is **inviting** her.

el lirio

1463　iris

Pancho siempre **plancha** toda su ropa.

1464　to iron

la plancha

1465　iron

el yelmo de **hierro**

1466　iron mask

la isla

1467　island

la picazón, la comezón

Marisol tocó una ortiga y ahora tiene una terrible **picazón**.
La comezón desaparece siempre y cuando no te rasques.

Marisol got a bad itch from poison ivy.
The itch will go away if she does not scratch.

1468　itch

picar

1469　to itch

Me pica todo el cuerpo.

1470　My skin is **itchy**.

La hiedra sube por las paredes.

1471　ivy

J

Enrique me **dio un codazo**.
1472   to jab

Como verán, esta **chaqueta** no es mía . . .
1473   jacket

el forro, la sobrecubierta
1474   dust jacket

un borde **mellado, dentado**
1475   jagged edge

la cárcel
1476   jail/gaol*

la mermelada
1477   jam

atascar
1478   to jam

Enero es el primer mes del año.
1479   January

el jarro, el pote, el frasco
1480   jar

Los tiburones tienen unas **mandíbulas** horribles.
1481   jaw

el pantalón vaquero, los jeans
1482   jeans

el jeep, el yip, el jip
1483   jeep

De postre tenemos **jalea**.
1484   jelly

motor a **chorro**, motor a **reacción**
1485   jet engine

avión a reacción, avión a chorro
1486   jet plane

la joya, la alhaja
1488   jewel

el rompecabezas
1489   jigsaw puzzle

Ricardo está haciendo **un trabajo**.
1490   doing a job

un chorro de agua
1487   jet of water

Un jockey es **un jinete** de caballos de carrera.

1491   jockey

trotar

1492   to jog

Hay que **juntar** las dos partes.

1493   to join

la articulación del codo

1494   joint

El pesado de Torcuato cree que sus **bromas** son buenas.

1495   joke

El juez va a dictar su fallo.

1496   judge

el malabarista

1497   juggler

el jugo, el zumo de naranja

1498   juice

¿Es **julio** buena época para ir a nadar?

1499   July

saltar

1500   to jump

saltar a

1501   to jump in

saltar a

1502   to jump on

Cristián es buen **saltador**.

1503   jumper

el jumper, el mono

1504   jumper/pinafore*

los cables de cierre o **puente**

1505   jumper cables/jump leads*

En **junio** juego al tenis.

1506   June

En **la selva** quedan pocos tigres.

1507   jungle

Un junco es un barco chino.

1508   junk

Los desechos quiere decir la basura.

1509   junk

acabar de, sólo, justo

Marisol **acaba de** llegar a casa.
Sólo un poquito, gracias.
Este juez es un hombre **justo**.

Marisol just got home.
Just a little, thanks.
The judge is a just person.

1510   just

K

el caleidoscopio
1511   kaleidoscope

el canguro
1512   kangaroo

la quilla
1513   keel

A Macabeo le gusta su **perrera**.
1514   kennel

el grano
1515   kernel

la tetera, la pava
1516   kettle

la llave
1517   key

patear, dar un puntapié
1518   to kick

Este **chiquillo** es amigo mío.
1519   kid

Las cabras recién nacidas se llaman **cabritos**.
1520   kid

El que **secuestra** a una persona es un criminal.
1521   to kidnap

el riñón
1522   kidney

Un cazador furtivo **mató** al pobre león.
1523   to kill

Los cacharros de greda se cuecen en **un horno**.
1524   kiln

1 **kilogramo** = 1000 gramos
1525   kilogram

1 **kilómetro** = 1000 metros
1526   kilometer/kilometre*

el faldellín escocés
1527   kilt

Un vestido es **un tipo** de ropa.
1528   A dress is a kind of garment.

una niñita muy **amable**
1529   kind girl

el rey

1530   king

el martín pescador

1531   kingfisher

el quiosco de la esquina

1532   kiosk

el pescado ahumado

1533   kippers

besar, besarse

1534   to kiss

el beso

1535   kiss

la cocina

1536   kitchen

el volantín, el papalote, el barrilete, la cometa

1537   kite

Los gatitos son muy retozones.

1538   kitten

El kiwi es una fruta muy sabrosa.

1539   kiwi

la rodilla

1540   knee

arrodillarse, hincarse

1541   to kneel

el cuchillo

1542   knife

Mamá me está **tejiendo** un chaleco de lana.

1543   to knit

la perilla, el pomo

1544   knob

Alguien **golpea** a la puerta.

1545   to knock

el nudo

1546   knot

saber, conocer

¿Tú **sabes** lo que eso quiere decir?
Conócete a ti mismo.

Do you know what it means?
Know yourself.

1547   to know

los nudillos

1548   knuckle

El oso **koala** vive en Australia.

1549   koala bear

L

La etiqueta dice que es un veneno mortal.

1550   label

el laboratorio

1551   laboratory

un cuello de **encaje**

1552   lace

la escalera de tijera

1554   ladder

el cucharón

1555   ladle

la señora, la dama

1556   lady

Orlando **se ata** los cordones.

1553   to lace

la mariquita, la chinita

1557   ladybug/ladybird*

los dedos de dama, las lenguas de gato

1558   ladyfingers

Esta es **la guarida** de un monstruo.

1559   lair

Los lagos están rodeados de tierra.

1560   lake

el cordero, el borrego

1561   lamb

Platero tiene una patita **coja**.

1562   lame

la lámpara

1563   lamp

el poste de alumbrado, el farol

1564   lamp-post

la lanza

1565   lance

la tierra firme

1566   land

aterrizar

1567   to land

el descanso, el rellano

1568   landing

el casero, el arrendador

El departamento en que vivimos es de mi **casero**.
El arrendador nos cobra un alquiler mensual.

The apartment we live in belongs to our landlord.
We pay our landlord rent every month.

1569 landlord

Algunas carreteras tienen cuatro **pistas**.

1570 lane

el idioma, la lengua, el lenguaje

¿Cuántos **idiomas** sabes hablar?
La lengua materna de Marisol es el castellano.
Los abogados usan **un lenguaje** muy complicado.

How many languages can you speak?
Spanish is Marisol's first language.
Lawyers use very complicated language.

1571 language

el farol, la lámpara

1572 lantern

un niño sentado en **el regazo** de su mamá

1573 lap

el alerce

1574 larch

la manteca

1575 lard

grande

1576 large

la alondra

1577 lark

la pestaña

1578 lash

el **último** pedazo

1579 the **last** piece

Algunas cosas **perduran** a través de los siglos.

1580 Some things do **last**.

Deja **cerrado con pestillo**, por favor.

1581 to **latch**

Llegas **retrasado**.

1582 You are **late**.

la espuma de afeitar

1583 lather

reír, reírse

1584 to laugh

Los Padilla bajaron a tierra en **una lancha**.

1585 launch

lanzar

1586 to launch

la plataforma de lanzamiento

1587 launchpad

la ropa sucia

1588 laundry/washing*

Liliana lava su ropa sucia en una **lavandería**.

1589   laundry/launderette*

la lavanda

1590   lavender

¡Respeta **la ley**!

1591   Obey the law!

¿Te gusta cortar **el césped**?

1592   lawn

poner baldosas

1594   to **lay** tiles

un pastel con varias **capas** de crema

1595   **layer** upon **layer**

¡Qué tipo más **holgazán**!

1596   He is **lazy**.

la cortadora de pasto

1593   lawn mower

Fidel **lleva** al caballo de las riendas.

1597   to **lead**

el jefe del grupo

1598   leader

la hoja

1599   leaf

Este balde **gotea**.

1600   to **leak**

Esta torre **se inclina** más todos los años.

1601   to **lean**

Yo **aprendo** a leer.

1602   I **learn** to read.

la correa, la traílla

1603   leash/lead*

Casi todos los zapatos se hacen de **cuero**.

1604   Shoes are made of **leather**.

Te lo **dejo** aquí.

1605   to **leave**

Víctor **se va**.

1606   to **leave**

el antepecho de mi ventana

1607   **ledge** of a window

el puerro

1608   leek

1609 — Al llegar a la esquina dobla a **la izquierda**. — left

1610 — Yo soy **zurdo**. ¿Y tú? — He is left-handed.

1611 — Todos tenemos **piernas**. — leg

1612 — ¿Conoces **la leyenda** de los Cíclopes? — legend

1613 — **el limón** — lemon

1614 — **la limonada** — lemonade

1615 — Te voy a **prestar** este libro. — to lend

1616 — **el lente, el cristal** — lens

1617 — **El leopardo** es un felino. — leopard

1618 — **la malla** — leotard

1619 — En este montoncito hay **menos**. — There is less here.

1620 — Este sabio me enseñó **una lección**. — lesson

1621 — ¡**Suéltame**! ¡**Déjame** ir! — Let me go!

1622 — la primera **letra** del alfabeto — letter of the alphabet

1623 — Marisol escribió **una carta** a su abuelita. — letter

1624 — **la lechuga** — lettuce

1625 — una superficie **nivelada** — level surface

1626 — **la palanca** — lever

1627 — Más rápido se pilla a **un mentiroso** que a un ladrón. — liar

1628 — En **las bibliotecas** hay que guardar silencio. — library

la matrícula, la patente, la placa

1629   licence plate/number plate*

lamer

1630   to lick

la tapa del frasco

1631   lid

Para **mentir** y comer pescado . . .

1632   to lie

Acaba de empezar su **vida**.

1634   life

el bote salvavidas

1635   lifeboat

levantar, alzar

1636   to lift

recostarse, acostarse, echarse

1633   to lie down

Enciende **la luz**.

1637   light/table lamp*

Papá **prende** una vela.

1638   to light

la ampolleta, la bombilla

1639   lightbulb

Una buena forma de **aligerar** la carga.

1640   She **lightens** the load.

el faro

1641   lighthouse

rayos y truenos

1642   lightning

el pararrayos

1643   lightning rod

A Pepita le **gustan** los gatos.

1644   to like

probable, apropiado

Lo más **probable** es que Consuelo no venga mañana.
Este es un lugar **apropiado** para pescar.

Consuelo is not likely to come tomorrow.
This is a likely place to fish.

1645   likely

Las lilas florecen en la primavera.

1646   lilac

azucenas de Semana Santa

1647   lily

una rama de árbol

1648   limb

la lima

1649   lime

el límite

Hay **un límite** de tres artículos por cliente.
El límite de velocidad es de 50 kilómetros por hora.
La gentileza de Orlando no tiene **límites**.

There is a limit of three items per customer.
The speed limit is 50 kilometers per hour.
There is no limit to Orlando's kindness.

1650   limit

Mi vecino **cojea** al andar.

1651   to limp

¿Sabes dibujar **líneas** rectas?

1652   line

la ropa blanca, la lencería, la ropa de cama

1653   linen

el transatlántico

1654   liner

Mi casaca tiene **un forro** muy abrigador.

1655   lining

enlazar

1656   to link

las hilachas, las pelusas

1657   lint

el león

1658   lion

los labios

1659   lips

el lápiz labial, la barra de labios

1660   lipstick

Tanto el agua como la leche son **líquidos**.

1661   liquid

la lista de las compras

1662   list

Están **escuchando** un recital.

1663   They are **listening**.

un litro

1664   liter/litre*

Ensuciar la calle está muy mal.

1665   to **litter**

una manzana **pequeña, una manzanita**

1666   a **little** apple

vivir

Marisol **vive** en una ciudad.
Tía María **vive** de su jubilación.
Vivir en el planeta Marte sería muy difícil.

Marisol lives in the city.
Aunt Maria lives on a pension.
It would be difficult to live on Mars.

1667   to **live**

vivaracha, vivaz

1668   lively

la sala, el salón, la sala de estar

1669   living room/lounge*

la lagartija

1670   lizard

Martín **cargó** el cañón.

1671   to load

Los obreros **cargan** un camión.

1672   to load

la hogaza de pan, **el pan**

1673   loaf

prestar

Emiliano le **prestó** dinero a Marisol después de que ella gastó toda su mesada.

Emiliano loaned Marisol some money because she had spent her allowance.

1674   to loan/lend*

un tipo de **langosta** . . .

1675   lobster

¿ **Le echaste llave** a la puerta?

1676   to lock

la locomotora

1678   locomotive

. . . y otro tipo de **langosta.**

1679   locust

un albergue en la montaña

1680   lodge/chalet*

una puerta con **cerradura**

1677   lock

el altillo, la buhardilla

1681   loft

el tronco, el leño

1682   log

la paleta, el chupetín

1683   lollipop

solitario

1684   lonely

Las jirafas tienen un cuello muy **largo.**

1685   long

mirar

1686   to look

Marisol teje una bufanda en **el telar.**

1687   loom

un lazo en la amarra

1688   loop

El reloj me queda suelto.

1689 loose

A Víctor se le perdió un guante.

1690 to lose

un poco de loción para la piel

1691 lotion

La música muy fuerte me da dolor de cabeza.

1692 loud

el altavoz, el parlante, el megáfono

1693 loudspeaker

holgazanear, flojear

1694 to lounge

el amor

El amor es algo muy importante. Marisol dice que el que tiene amor lo tiene todo.

Love is very important. Marisol says that if you have love you have everything.

1695 love

Nosotros nos queremos mucho.

1696 to love

preciosa, amorosa

1697 lovely

una ramita baja

1698 low branch

bajar

1699 to lower

afortunado

Raúl es afortunado de tener tan buenos amigos. ¡Qué tipo más afortunado!

Raul is lucky to have such good friends. What a lucky dog!

1700 lucky

el equipaje

1701 luggage

El agua tibia no está ni fría ni caliente.

1702 lukewarm water

La mamá canta una canción de cuna a su bebé.

1703 lullaby

la madera

1704 lumber/timber*

el chichón

1705 lump

el almuerzo

1706 lunch

la lonchera, la fiambrera

1707 lunchbox

Fumar daña los pulmones.

1708 lung

la revista

1709　magazine

Los gusanos no son muy agradables.

1710　maggot

un acto de **magia** un tanto diferente

1711　magic

el imán

1713　magnet

el **magnífico** manto del rey de la selva

1714　magnificent

la lupa

1715　magnifying glass

el mago

1712　magician

la urraca

1716　magpie

enviar por correo

1717　to mail/post*

el cartero

1718 mail carrier/postman*

Gustavo está **haciendo** un avioncito.

1719　to make

A Soledad le gusta usar **maquillaje**.

1720　makeup

el macho y la hembra

1721　male

el mazo

1722　mallet

el hombre y la mujer

1723　man

Al **mandarín** le gustan **las mandarinas**.

1724　mandarin

la mandolina

1725　mandolin

La melena de los caballos se llama **crin**.

1726　mane

El mango es una fruta muy dulce.

1727　mango

un señor de muy buenos **modales**
1728 He has good **manners.**

varios, muchos
1729 many

el mapa
1730 map

una escultura en **mármol**
1731 marble

marchar
1733 to march

El tercer mes del año se llama **marzo.**
1734 March

La hembra del caballo se llama **yegua.**
1735 mare

las canicas, las bolitas
1732 marbles

la caléndula
1736 marigold

Marca la respuesta que te parezca correcta.
1737 to mark

¡Sacaste muy buenas **notas!**
1738 mark

Mi papá tiene un puesto en **el mercado.**
1739 market

casarse
1740 to marry

el pantano, la ciénaga
1741 marsh

moler papas
1742 to mash potatoes

la máscara, el antifaz
1743 mask

Los fieles de la balanza tienen **masas** diferentes.
1744 mass

Todos los veleros tienen **un mástil.**
1745 mast

Carolina ya **domina** el arte de la bicicleta.
1746 to master

el partido de tenis
1747 match

Jugar con **fósforos** es muy peligroso.

1748　match

las matemáticas

2
+2
4

1749　mathematics

la cuestión, la materia

Iris vuelve en **cuestión** de minutos.
Tener **materia** gris significa ser inteligente.

Iris will be back in a matter of minutes.
To have gray matter means to be smart.

1750　matter

el colchón

1751　mattress

Mayo es el quinto mes del año.

1752　May

acaso, quizás, tal vez

Acaso Marisol debiera quedarse en casa.
Quizás mamá sepa.
No te respondo ni que sí ni que no, sino que **tal vez**.

Maybe Marisol should stay home.
Maybe Mother knows.
The answer is not yes, and it is not no, it is maybe.

1753　maybe

el alcalde de mi pueblo

1754　mayor

Este es **un laberinto**.

1755　maze

Los prados tienen pasto y flores.

1756　meadow

el sabanero

1757　meadowlark

la comida

1758　meal

un tipo **malo**

1759　mean person

A casi todos nos da **el sarampión**.

1760　measles

medir

1 2 3 4 5 6

1761　to measure

la carne

1762　meat

el mecánico

1763　mechanic

Mafalda se ganó **una medalla** al mérito.

1764　medal

un remedio para el dolor de cabeza

1765　medicine

mediano

1766　medium

encontrarse

1767　to meet

Todos los lunes hay reunión de profesores.

1768   meeting

el melón

1769   melon

derretir, derretirse

1770   to melt

Este club tiene cuatro miembros.

1771   Our club has four members.

el menú, la carta, la lista, la minuta

1772   menu

la merced, la compasión

Quedamos a **merced** de los elementos.
Ese miserable no tuvo **compasión** con nadie.

We are at the mercy of the weather.
The bandit showed no mercy to anyone.

1773   mercy

la sirena

1774   mermaid

alegre, feliz

1775   merry

¡Qué desorden más espantoso!

1776   a real mess

Te traigo **un mensaje.**

1777   message

el mensajero

1778   messenger

Esta es una jarra de **metal.**

1779   metal

Los meteoritos provienen del espacio.

1780   meteorite

el medidor

1781   meter

Un metro equivale a unas 40 pulgadas.

1782   meter/metre*

el método

Marisol usa **un método** para aprender más rápido.
Un método es una forma de hacer las cosas.
Sus **métodos** no son muy ortodoxos.

Marisol has a method for learning quickly.
A method is a way of doing things.
His methods are not very orthodox.

1783   method

el metrónomo

1784   metronome

Ricardo prefiere cantar con **micrófono.**

1785   microphone

el microscopio

1786   microscope

el horno de **microondas**

1787   microwave oven

el mediodía

1788   midday

en el medio

1789   in the middle

el enano

1790   midget

la medianoche

1791   midnight

la milla

Una **milla** equivale a 1,6 kilómetros.
El límite de velocidad es de 30 **millas** por hora.

One mile equals 1.6 kilometers.
The speed limit is 30 miles per hour.

1792   mile

la leche

1793   milk

el molino

1794   mill

una mente brillante

$E = MC^2$

1795   mind

una mina subterránea

1796   mine

Los mineros trabajan duro.

1797   miner

los minerales

1798   minerals

el pececillo

1799   minnow

la menta, la hierbabuena

1800   mint

¿Cuánto es siete **menos** cinco?

$7 - 5 = 2$

1801   minus

Un minuto tiene sesenta segundos.

1802   minute

Un milagro que funcionó al revés.

1803   miracle

un espejismo en el desierto

1804   mirage

el espejo

1805   mirror

Los avaros no convidan a nadie.

1806   miser

Extraño tanto a mi familia.

1807   to miss

el proyectil, el misil

1808   missile

Ignacio se extravió en **la niebla**.

1809   mist

el muérdago

1810   mistletoe

los mitones

1811   mittens

mezclar

1812   to mix

la batidora

1813   mixer

Los castillos de antaño tenían **un foso**.

1814   moat

burlarse

1815   to mock

el sinsonte

1816   mockingbird

un avioncito a **escala**

1817   model airplane/aeroplane*

un sillón **moderno**

1818   modern chair

¡Este niño tiene los pañales **mojados**!

1819   moist

el topo

1820   mole

Tengo **un lunar** en la cara.

1821   mole

Un **momento,** por favor.

1822   One moment please.

el lunes

El lunes es el primer día de la semana.
Todos los lunes Marisol se levanta temprano.

Monday is the first day of the week.
Every Monday, Marisol gets up early.

1823   Monday

el dinero

1824   money

El mono desciende del árbol.

1825   monkey

Este es un tipo de tiburón llamado **angelote**.

1826   monkfish

el monstruo

1827   monster

El año tiene doce **meses**.	Más vale hacer **un monumento** a la verdad.
1828 month	**1829** monument
de buen **humor** . . .	. . . y de mal **genio**
1830 He is in a good **mood**.	**1831** He is in a bad **mood**.

la luna creciente	**el alce**
1832 moon	**1833** moose
la mañana	**El mortero** sirve para machacar.
1834 morning	**1835** mortar and pestle

el mosaico	**el mosquito**
1836 mosaic	**1837** mosquito
el musgo, el moho	**la madre**
1838 moss	**1839** mother

el motor eléctrico	**la motocicleta, la moto**
1840 motor	**1841** motorcycle
el molde para tortas	**un montículo** de tierra
1842 mould*/mold	**1843** mound

Cada cual **se monta** como quiere.	**la montaña**
1844 to mount	**1845** mountain
el ratón, la laucha	**el bigote, el mostacho**
1846 mouse	**1847** moustache*/mustache

la boca

1848   mouth

Los caracoles **se mueven** muy despacito.

1849   to move

¿Existirá la máquina de **movimiento** perpetuo?

1850   movement

el cine, el teatro

1851   movie/film*

cortar el pasto

1852   to **mow** the lawn

Esto es **mucho** para una sola persona.

1853   too **much** for me

¿Pero qué haces sentado en **el barro**?

1854   mud

la mula, el mulo

1855   mule

multiplicar

1856   multiply

las paperas

1857   mumps

Asesinar a alguien es un crimen horrendo.

1858   to murder

Los luchadores tienen grandes **músculos**.

1859   muscle

el museo

1860   museum

Algunos **hongos** son muy venenosos.

1861   mushroom

Marisol es muy aficionada a **la música**.

1862   music

La mamá de Marisol es **músico**.

1863   musician

Los mejillones son invertebrados.

1864   mussel

Usted perdone, pero **tiene que** saltar. . .

1865   You **must** jump.

la mostaza

1866   mustard

el bozal

1867   muzzle

N

el clavo

1868   nail

la uña

1869   finger**nail**

el cortaúñas

1870   **nail** clipper

desnudos, en cueros, piluchos, calatos

1872   naked

Mi **nombre** es . . .

1873   My **name** is...

la servilleta

1874   napkin/serviette*

clavar

1871   to **nail**

Está tan **angosto** que no alcanzo a pasar.

1875   too **narrow** to pass

Una nación es lo mismo que un país.

1876   nation

natural

Comer alimentos **naturales** es muy bueno para la salud.
Es importante proteger los recursos **naturales**.
Es muy **natural** que llore un recién nacido.

It is healthy to eat natural foods.
It is important to protect natural resources.
It is very natural that a newborn should cry.

1877   natural

Cuida siempre **la naturaleza**.

1878   nature

una niña **revoltosa**

1879   She is **naughty**.

Antes se **navegaba** según las estrellas.

1880   to **navigate**

Ya está llegando **cerca** . . .

1881   near

pulcro, aseado

1882   neat

No es muy agradable, pero es **necesario**.

1883 Not pleasant, but **necessary**.

el cuello

1884   neck

el collar

1885   necklace

La venganza es **el néctar** de los dioses.

1886   nectar

**el melocotón,
el durazno pelado**

1887   nectarine

el apuro, la carencia

Marisol siempre ayuda a un amigo en **apuros**.
En el desierto hay una gran **carencia** de agua.

Marisol always helps her friends in need.
There is a great need for water in the desert.

1888   need

¡Dios mío, **necesito** un vaso de agua!

1889   I need water.

¿Sabes enhebrar **una aguja**?

1890   needle

El que **descuida** a su perro no merece tenerlo.

1891   He neglects his dog.

Las vacas mugen, los caballos **relinchan**.

1892   to neigh

los vecinos

1893   neighbors/neighbours*

Ninguno de los dos me queda bien.

1894   neither one fits

un letrero de neón

1895   neon sign

Mi **sobrino** es el hijo de mi hermano.

1896   My nephew is my brother's son.

Los nervios son parte del sistema nervioso.

1897   nerve

Toti se siente un poco **nervioso**.

1898   nervous

Se ven dos huevitos en **el nido**.

1899   nest

La ortiga pica como diablo.

1900   nettle

¡Nunca juegues con fuego!

1901   Never play with fire!

nuevo

1902   new

la noticia, la nueva, la novedad

Mamá lee **las noticias**.
Tenemos buenas **nuevas**.
¿Has tenido **novedades** de tu casa?

Mom reads the news.
The news is good.
Any news from home?

1903   news

el diario, el periódico

1904   newspaper

**¡El siguiente!
¡El próximo!**

1905   Next !

Las ardillas siempre **mordisquean** la comida.

1906   to nibble

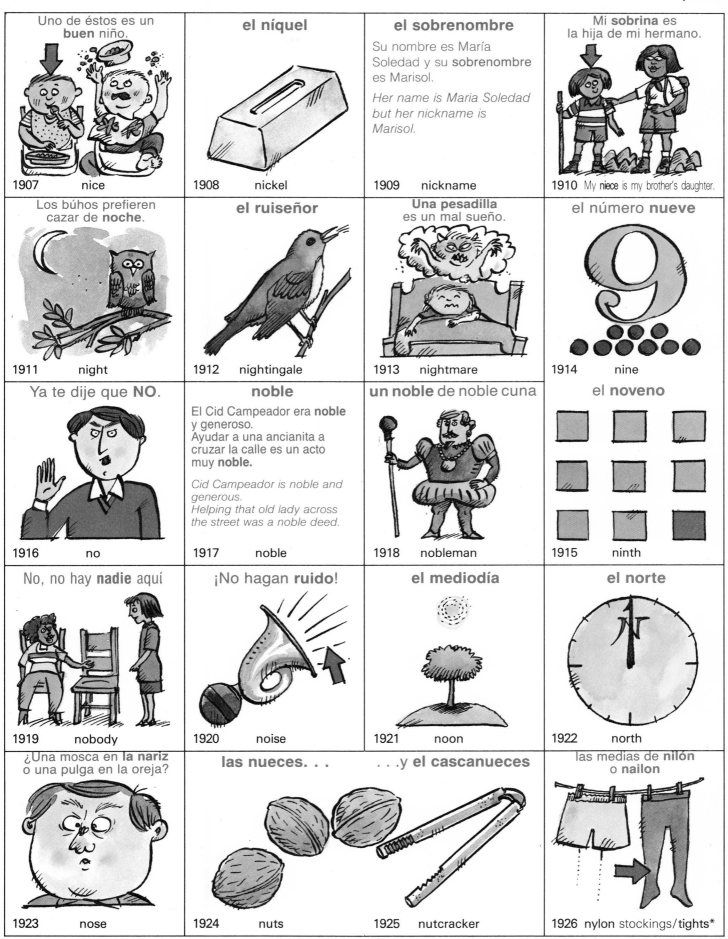

Uno de éstos es un **buen** niño.

1907   nice

el níquel

1908   nickel

el sobrenombre

Su nombre es María Soledad y su **sobrenombre** es Marisol.

Her name is Maria Soledad but her nickname is Marisol.

1909   nickname

Mi **sobrina** es la hija de mi hermano.

1910   My **niece** is my brother's daughter.

Los búhos prefieren cazar de **noche**.

1911   night

el ruiseñor

1912   nightingale

Una **pesadilla** es un mal sueño.

1913   nightmare

el número **nueve**

1914   nine

Ya te dije que **NO**.

1916   no

noble

El Cid Campeador era **noble** y generoso.
Ayudar a una ancianita a cruzar la calle es un acto muy **noble.**

Cid Campeador is noble and generous.
Helping that old lady across the street was a noble deed.

1917   noble

un noble de noble cuna

1918   nobleman

el **noveno**

1915   ninth

No, no hay **nadie** aquí

1919   nobody

¡No hagan **ruido**!

1920   noise

el mediodía

1921   noon

el norte

1922   north

¿Una mosca en **la nariz** o una pulga en la oreja?

1923   nose

las nueces. . .

. . .y el cascanueces

1924   nuts

1925   nutcracker

las medias de **nilón** o **nailon**

1926   nylon stockings/**tights***

el roble, la encina

1927 oak

Un tiburón aficionado a **los remos** . . .

1928 oar

un oasis en medio del desierto

1929 oasis

apaisado, oblongo

1930 oblong

observar

1931 to observe

En **el océano** viven la mar de peces.

1932 ocean

Un octógono tiene ocho lados.

1933 octagon

Octubre se llama el décimo mes del año.

1934 October

el pulpo

1935 octopus

El cuentakilómetros sirve para eso mismo.

1936 odometer/milometer*

el olor

1937 odor/odour*

raro, fuera, apagado

Esta comida tiene un gusto **raro**.
La música está **fuera** de tono.
La luz está **apagada**.

This food tastes off.
The music is off key.
The light is off.

1938 off

Yo le **ofrezco** un mejor precio por la vaca.

1939 to offer

el oficial

1940 officer

frecuentemente, a menudo, con frecuencia

Frecuentemente Marisol hace preguntas complicadas.
No vengo por aquí **a menudo**.
¿Con qué **frecuencia** salen los trenes?

Marisol often asks difficult questions.
I don't come here often.
How often does the train run?

1941 often

el aceite

1942 oil

el unguento, la pomada

1943 ointment

un señor muy **viejo** con unas alas enormes

1944 old

El árbol de **la aceituna** se llama olivo.

1945 olive

Para hacer **una tortilla** hay que quebrar huevos.

1946   omelette

El florero está **encima de** la mesa.

1947   **on** the table

una vez

Erase **una vez**, que había una niñita llamada Marisol . . .
He visto esta película más de **una vez**.

Once upon a time, there was a little girl called Marisol . . .
I have seen this movie more than once.

1948   once

el número **uno**

1949   one

la cebolla

1950   onion

Tú eres mi **único** amor.

1951   my **only** love

No dejes la puerta **abierta**.

1952   open

abrir

1953   to **open**

la operación

1954   operation

la zarigüeya

1955   opossum

en frente de, contrario, opuesto

Los Zenteno viven **en frente de** nosotros.
El bien es **lo contrario** del mal.
Cada uno partió en dirección **opuesta**.

The Zentenos live opposite us.
Good is the opposite of bad.
We went in opposite directions.

1956   opposite

o, u

¿Puedo entrar, **o** estás ocupado?
Entregue detalles sobre su profesión **u** oficio.

Can I come in or are you busy?
Provide details about your profession or trade.

1957   or

la naranja

1958   orange

el color **naranja, anaranjado**

1959   orange

En **los huertos** hay árboles frutales.

1960   orchard

la orquesta

1961   orchestra

la orquídea

1962   orchid

¿Puedo **pedir** mi comida?

1963   to order

el orégano

1964   oregano

un órgano de iglesia

1965   organ

la oropéndola

1966   oriole

Un huérfano no tiene padres.

1967   orphan

Las avestruces no pueden volar.

1968   ostrich

Las nutrias son muy juguetonas.

1969   otter

Una libra tiene dieciséis **onzas**.

1970   ounce

¿A quién no le gusta andar al **aire libre**?

1971   outdoors

¿Te gusta mi **indumentaria**?

1972   outfit

ovalado

1973   oval

En la puerta del **horno** se quema el pan.

1974   oven

¡Hombre **al agua**!

1975   Man overboard!

el sobretodo, el abrigo, el **gabán**

1976   overcoat

desbordar, rebosar, derramarse

1977   to **overflow**

el chanclo, la galocha

1978   overshoe

darse vuelta de campana, volcarse

1979   to **overturn**

deber

Ustedes le **deben** respeto a la maestra.
Lo mejor es no **deberle** dinero a nadie.

You owe respect to your teacher.
It is best not to owe any money.

1980   to **owe**

la lechuza, el búho

1981   owl

tener, ser dueño de

Nosotros **tenemos** casa propia.
Los Zenteno **son dueños de** una cabañita cerca del lago.

We own our house.
The Zentenos own a cottage on the lake.

1982   to **own**

el buey

1983   ox

el oxígeno

1984   oxygen

Algunas **ostras** traen una perla adentro.

1985   oyster

P

Marisol **empaca** su mochila:

1986　　to pack

el paquete

1987　　package

Alguien estuvo usando mi **bloc** de papel.

1988　　pad

Georgina va remando con **un canalete** . . .

1990　　paddle

. . . pero todavía no sabe **remar** muy bien.

1991　　to paddle

el candado

1992　　padlock

la plataforma de lanzamiento

1989　　pad

Demos vuelta **la página**.

1993　　page

un balde de agua para abrevar los caballos

1994　　pail

la pintura

1996　　paint

No es muy astuto tocar **la pintura** fresca.

1997　　wet paint

Martín se lastimó un dedo y siente mucho **dolor.**

1995　　pain

el pintor de brocha gorda

2000　　painter

Tía Irma le pidió a Martín que **pintara** la cerca.

1998　　to paint

la brocha

1999　　paintbrush

la pintura, el cuadro

2001　　painting

un par de zapatillas

2002　　a pair of shoes

el palacio

2003　　palace

Esta flor es de un tono más bien **pálido.**

2004　　pale

la paleta	Yo conozco mi ciudad como **la palma** de mi mano.	**la fuente**	A Marisol le encantan **los panqueques**.
2005 palette	2006 palm	2007 pan	2008 pancake
el oso **panda**	**el tablero** de instrumentos	**la zampoña**	**el pensamiento**
2009 panda	2010 panel	2011 panpipe	2012 pansy
jadear, acezar	**¿La pantera** rosa?	**los pantalones**	**la papaya**
2013 to pant	2014 panther	2015 pants/trousers*	2016 papaya
el papel	**el paracaídas**	**el desfile, la parada**	**unas líneas paralelas**
2017 paper	2018 parachute	2019 parade	2020 parallel lines
El ratoncito quedó **paralizado** de miedo.	El cartero trajo **un paquete** para Marisol.	Yo quiero mucho a mis **padres**.	A la abuela le gustan **los parques**.
2021 paralyzed/paralysed*	2022 parcel	2023 parent	2024 park

El papá de Marisol siempre **estaciona** aquí.

2025   to park

la parka

2026   parka

En **el Parlamento** se hacen las leyes.

2027   parliament

Los loros son muy parlanchines.

2028   parrot

el perejil

2029   parsley

La pastinaca es una hortaliza europea.

2030   parsnip

En el aire siempre hay **partículas** de polvo.

2031   particle

Javier es buena **pareja** de baile.

2032   partner

A Marisol le encantan **las fiestas**.

2033   party

Pilar **pasó** la pelota tan mal. . .

2034   to pass

. . . que su hermano **se desmayó**.

2035   to pass out

el pasadizo

2036   passage

el pasajero

2037   passenger

Para sacar una visa hace falta **un pasaporte**.

2038   passport

el pasado

En **el pasado** no habían ni autos ni aviones.
El pretérito es el **pasado** de un verbo.

In the past, there were no planes or cars.
The preterit is a verb's past tense.

2039   past

Si comes muchos **fideos** te pones gordo.

2040   pasta

El papel mural se **empasta** con engrudo.

2041   to paste

El bordado es uno de **los pasatiempos** de mamá.

2042   pastime

¿A quién no le gustan **los pasteles**?

2043   pastry

Las ovejas pacen en **los pastizales**.

2044   pasture

Este **remiendo** lo puse yo mismo.

2045   patch

el sendero

2046   path

Marisol es una niña muy **paciente**.

2047   She is patient.

un paciente asustado

2048   patient

el molde, el patrón para un vestido

2049   pattern

detenerse, hacer una pausa
Después de leer un par de páginas, Marisol **se detuvo** por unos segundos.
La partitura indica que el pianista **hace una pausa**.

After reading two pages, Marisol paused for a few seconds.
The score shows that the pianist must pause.

2050   to pause

caminar sobre **el pavimento**

2051   pavement/road*

¿Cuántas **garras** tiene un gato?

2052   paw

Todo el mundo vive **pagando** cuentas.

2053   to pay

el teléfono público

2054 pay phone/phone box*

paz en la tierra

2055   peace

el durazno, el melocotón

2056   peach

el pavo real

2057   peacock

la cima, la cumbre

2058   peak

Se oye **un repique** de campanas.

2059   peal of a bell

el maní, el cacahuete

2060   peanut

la pera

2061   pear

la perla

2062   pearl

las arvejas, los guisantes

2063   peas

La turba ayuda a las plantas a crecer.

2064   peat moss

Demóstenes se ponía **guijarros** en la boca.

2065   pebbles

La pacana es una nuez de norteamérica.

2066   pecan

picotear

2067   to peck

el pedal

2068   pedal

el peatón

2070   pedestrian

el cruce de peatones

2071   pedestrian crossing

pelar

2072   to peel

pedalear

2069   to pedal

el pelícano

2073   pelican

la pluma, el bolígrafo

2074   pen

el lápiz

2075   pencil

el reloj de péndulo

2076   pendulum

el pingüino, el pájaro bobo

2077   penguin

el cortaplumas

2078   penknife

El pentágono tiene cinco lados.

2079   pentagon

un grupo de gente

2080   people

el molinillo de **pimienta**

2081   pepper

la menta

2082   peppermint

la perca

2083   perch

El pajarillo posado en **la percha**.

2084   perch

una gran **actuación**

2085 performance

el perfume

2086 perfume

El punto se pone al final de una frase.

glurg.

2087 period/full stop*

la pervinca

2088 periwinkle

la persona

2089 person

la plaga

2090 pest

Mauricio **importuna** a su papá.

2091 to pester

una mascota fuera de lo común

2092 pet

Las flores tienen **pétalos**.

2094 petal

la petunia

2095 petunia

Los boticarios despachan recetas.

2096 pharmacist/chemist*

Al perrito le gusta que le **hagan cariño**.

2093 to pet

la farmacia, la botica

2097 pharmacy/chemist's*

el faisán

2098 pheasant

el teléfono

2099 phone

la fotografía

2100 photograph

el piano

2101 piano

Escoge una carta.

2102 to pick

Angélica **levanta** la muñeca.

2103 to pick up

el pico, el zapapico

2104 pickaxe

escabeche

2105   pickles

Marisol aprendió a **escabechar** cebollitas.

2106   to pickle

el picnic

2107   picnic

Orlando pinta **cuadros** modernos.

2108   picture

Me gusta **el pastel** de choclo . . .

2109   pie

. . . pero no me dieron más que **un pedazo**.

2110   a piece/slice* of pie

juntar, pegar los pedazos

2111   to piece together

el muelle de embarque

2112   pier

el cerdo, el chancho, el puerco, el marrano, el cochino

2113   pig

la paloma, el pichón

2114   pigeon

el chiquero, la porqueriza

2115   pigsty

el montón de tierra

2116   pile

Las píldoras las receta el doctor.

2117   pill/tablet*

el pilar

2118   pillar

A los gatos les encantan **los almohadones**.

2119   pillow

la funda de almohada

2120   pillowcase

Sin **piloto** no vuela el avión.

2121   pilot

la espinilla

2122   pimple

las pinzas, las tenazas

2123   pincers

A mí me gusta **pellizcar** a mi hermana.

2124   to pinch

el pino

2125   pine

la piña, el ananá

2126   pineapple

rosado, el color **rosa**

2127   pink

la pipa

2128   pipe

el pirata

2129   pirate

el pistacho

2130   pistachio

una pistola antigua

2131   pistol

Sergio **lanza** la pelota.

2132   to pitch

sentir lástima

Al pobre niño se le perdió su gatito y Marisol **siente** mucha **lástima** por él.

Marisol pities the poor boy who lost his cat.

2136   to pity

el lugar, la casa

¡Liliana, nos equivocamos de **lugar**!
¿Quieres venir a nuestra **casa**?

Liliana, we are in the wrong place!
Would you like to come to our place?

2137   place

la platija, la acedía

2138   plaice

el tiro, el tono

¡Buen **tiro**, Sergio!
Esta canción está fuera de **tono**.

Hey Sergio, that was a good pitch!
This song is off pitch.

2133   pitch

una camisa
sin adornos, lisa

2139   plain shirt

el llano, la llanura

2140   plain

planificar, proyectar

2141   to plan

la horquilla

2134   pitchfork

el cepillo de carpintero

2142   plane

Los planetas giran
en torno al Sol.

2143   planets

el tablón

2144   plank

la brea, el alquitrán

2135   pitch tar

las plantas / **plantar**		**el yeso**	Gabriela está **enluciendo** la pared con yeso.
2145 plants / 2146 to plant		2147 plaster	2148 to plaster

el plástico	**la plasticina**	Marisol siempre come en su **plato** favorito.	**la meseta, la altiplanicie**
2149 plastic	2150 plasticine	2151 plate	2152 plateau

el andén del ferrocarril	**jugar**	**el patio de juegos**	**el naipe, la carta**
2153 platform	2154 to play	2155 playground	2156 playing cards

suplicar, implorar	un día muy **agradable**	Un vaso de leche, **por favor**.	La falda escocesa tiene muchos **pliegues**.
2157 to plead	2158 a pleasant day	2159 A glass of milk, **please**.	2160 pleat

los alicates	**el arado**	**arrancar, desplumar**	**el enchufe**
2161 pliers	2162 plow/plough*	2163 to pluck	2164 plug

el tapón

2165   plug

la ciruela

2166   plum

la plomera, la fontanera

2167   plumber

rollizo, rechoncho, regordete

2168   plump

el plural

"Uno" es singular,
"muchos" es **plural**.
Niños es **el plural** de niño.

"One" is singular, "many" is plural.
Children is the plural of child.

2169   plural

Uno más uno da . . .

2170   plus

la madera terciada

2171   plywood

el chef Jacques escalfando huevos

2172   to poach

el bolsillo

2173   pocket

la vaina de arvejas

2174   pea pod

el poema

Hoy escribí **un poema** para mi mamá diciéndole que la quiero para siempre jamás.

2175   poem

apuntar con el dedo es mala educación

2177   to point

la flor de Pascua, la flor de fuego

2176   poinsettia

el veneno

2180   poison

ponzoñoso, venenoso

Algunos insectos tienen una picada **ponzoñosa**. No existen muchas serpientes **venenosas**.

Some insects have a poisonous sting. There are not many poisonous snakes.

2181   poisonous

una punta muy afilada

2178   point

picar, aguijonear

2182   to poke

el oso polar

2183   polar bear

el poste

2184   pole

puntiagudo

2179   pointed

el policía
2185　policeman

la mujer policía
2186　policewoman

pulir, bruñir, lustrar
2187　to polish

atento, bien educado, cortés
Martín es muy **atento**.
Las personas **bien educadas** ceden su asiento en el bus.
Hernán Cortés no era muy **cortés**.

Martin is a very polite child.
Polite people give up their seat on the bus.
Hernan Cortes was not very polite.

2188　polite

el polen
2189　pollen

la granada
2190　pomegranate

el estanque
2191　pond

el caballito, el poni
2192　pony

la piscina, la pileta, la alberca
2193　pool

Los vecinos **aunaron** sus esfuerzos.
2194　to pool

deficiente, pobre
Marisol tuvo notas muy **deficientes** este semestre.
Pobre diablo, se le perdió su cachimba.

Marisol had very poor marks this term.
Poor devil, he lost his pipe.

2195　poor

saltar, reventar, estallar
2196　to pop

el álamo
2197　poplar

la amapola
2198　poppy

popular
A Marisol no le gusta la música **popular**.
Este es un libro muy **popular**.

Marisol dislikes popular music.
This book is very popular.

2199　popular

Memo sale al **porche** por las tardes.
2200　porch

Los poros son agujeritos que tenemos en la piel.
2201　Pores are little holes in the skin.

avena cocida con leche
2202　porridge

el puerto
2203　port

portátil
Marisol está juntando su mesada para comprar una radio **portátil**.

Marisol wants a portable radio but she has not saved up enough money from her allowance.

2204　portable

el botones, el mozo de cuerda, el cargador

2205 porter

Este es un retrato de la Tía Adriana.

2206 portrait

el poste

2207 post

Orlando **despachó** una carta.

2208 to post

la tarjeta postal

2210 postcard

el cartel

2211 poster

la olla

2212 pot

la oficina de correos

2209 post office

la papa, la patata

2213 potato

los cacharros, la alfarería

2214 pottery

la bolsa, el saquito

2215 pouch

abalanzarse

2216 to pounce

la perrera, la libra
Los perros vagabundos van a parar a **la perrera**.
Cuatro plátanos pesan cerca de **una libra**.
La libra esterlina es la moneda de Inglaterra.
Stray dogs are taken to the dog pound.
Four bananas weigh about a pound.
The pound sterling is Britain's currency.

2217 pound

golpear, triturar, machacar

2218 to pound

verter, escanciar, vaciar, echar

2219 to pour

enfurruñarse, hacer pucheros

2220 to pout

los polvos talco

2221 powder

ensayar, practicar

2222 to practice/practise*

En **las praderas** se cultiva el trigo.

2223 prairie

elogiar, alabar

2224 to praise

Los caballos **corvetean**.	**rezar, orar**	Yo **prefiero** éste.	Esta señora está **embarazada**.
2225 to prance	2226 to pray	2227 to prefer	2228 She is pregnant.
¿González? ¡**Presente**, señor!	**el obsequio, el regalo** de cumpleaños	Tomás **hace entrega** del trofeo.	frutas en **conserva**
2229 I am present.	2230 birthday present	2231 to present	2232 preserved fruit
Apreta el botón.	**linda, bonita**	el búho y su **presa**	**el precio**
2233 to press	2234 pretty	2235 prey	2236 price
pinchar, pincharse	el bicho **espinudo**	**la escuela primaria**	**la primavera**
2237 to prick	2238 prickly animal	2239 primary school	2240 primrose
el príncipe	**la princesa**	**la directora** de mi escuela	**el principio**

el principio

Én **principio** estaría de acuerdo contigo.
La honestidad es una cuestión de **principios**.
Decir la verdad es un **principio** fundamental.

In principle, I agree with you.
Honesty is a matter of principle.
Truth is a sacred principle.

2241 prince	2242 princess	2243 school principal/Head teacher*	2244 principle

imprimir

2245   to print

La luz se descompone cuando pasa por **un prisma**.

2246   prism

Malandrín terminó en **prisión** por sus bellaquerías.

2247   prison

el preso, el prisionero

2248   prisoner

privado, particular, reservado

Marisol y yo tuvimos una conversación **privada**.
Martín toma clases **particulares**.
Él es una persona muy **reservada**.

Marisol and I are having a private talk.
Martin takes private lessons.
He is a very private person.

2249   private

Iris ganó el primer **premio** en el campeonato de natación.

2250   prize

el problema

2251   problem

frutas y verduras

2252   produce

La televisión pasa **programas** bastante mediocres.

2254   program/programme*

se prohibe, prohibido

2255   prohibited

el proyecto

Ximena está ocupada con **un proyecto**.
A Marisol le fue mal con su **proyecto**.

Ximena is working on a project.
Marisol did not do well on her project.

2256   project

Esta fábrica **produce** automóviles.

2253   This factory produces cars.

yo prometo, me comprometo

2257   I promise.

una horquilla de cuatro **puntas**

2258   prong

Cuando hables, **pronuncia** con claridad.

2259   to pronounce

Aquí está **la prueba** de que Micifuz se comió el canario.

2260   proof of guilt

apuntalar, sostener

2261   to prop

la hélice

2262   propeller

Ponte **bien** la ropa.

2263   properly dressed

la propiedad

Cuando Marisol dice ''esto es mío'', quiere decir ''esto es de mi **propiedad**''.
Su familia tiene **propiedades** en el campo.

Marisol says ''This is mine'' when she means ''This is my property''.
Her family owns property in the country.

2264   property

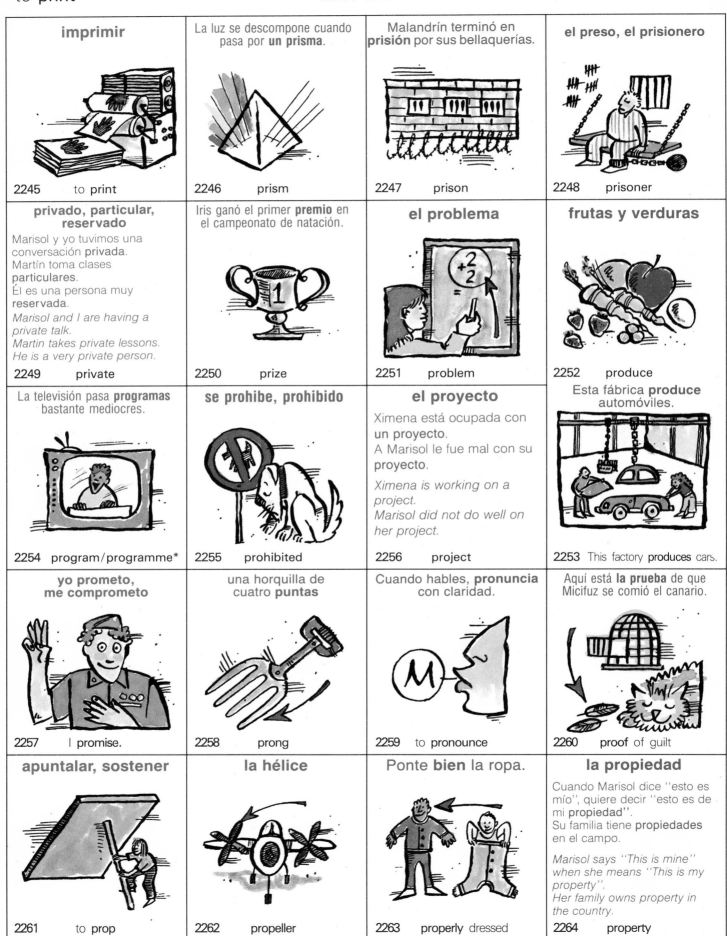

protestar

2265 to **protest**

un gato **orgulloso**

2266 I am a **proud** cat.

Usía, yo voy a **demostrar** que es así.

2267 to **prove**

el proverbio

Un antiguo **proverbio** chino:
"Cuando el río suena, es porque se cayó un piano al agua."
Here is a proverb:
"An apple a day keeps the doctor away."

2268 **proverb**

La escuela nos ha **proporcionado** sillas.

2269 to **provide** chairs

la ciruela pasa

2270 **prune**

podar

2271 to **prune**

el teléfono público

2272 **public** telephone/**phone box***

Tenemos **budín** de postre.

2273 **pudding/afters***

el charco, la poza

2274 **puddle**

dar bocanadas, **resoplar**

2275 to **puff**

el frailecillo

2276 **puffin**

tirar, jalar, halar

2277 to **pull**

la polea, la roldana

2278 **pulley**

el pulóver, el suéter

2279 **pullover/sweater***

El doctor me tomó **el pulso**.

2280 **pulse**

la bomba de agua

2281 **pump**

bombear

2282 to **pump**

el zapallo, la calabaza

2283 **pumpkin**

dar **puñetazos**

2284 to **punch**

Eres muy **puntual**.

2285 You are **punctual**.

Pinchar un neumático no es ninguna gracia.

2286 to puncture

castigar

2287 to punish

el castigo

2288 punishment

Pinocho es **un títere** de madera.

2289 puppet

el cachorro

2290 puppy

Ya no quedan muchos manantiales de agua **pura**.

2291 pure water

morado, púrpura

2292 purple

Los gatos **ronronean** cuando están contentos.

2293 to purr

el bolso, la cartera

2294 purse/handbag*

perseguir

2295 to pursue

empujar

2296 to push

Ponlo por aquí, por favor.

2297 to put

guardar

2298 to put away

Postergar los deberes no es buen método.

2299 to put off

La masilla afirma los vidrios.

2300 putty

el rompecabezas

2301 puzzle

el pijama, el piyama

2302 pyjamas*/pajamas

la pirámide

2303 pyramid

la serpiente **pitón**

2304 python

la codorniz

2305   quail

un reloj de **calidad**

2306   **quality** watch

una taza para medir **cantidades**

2307   quantity

pelear, reñir

2308   to quarrel

El mármol y la piedra salen de **las canteras**.

2309   quarry

un cuarto

$\frac{1}{4}$

2310   quarter

Un bote llegó al **embarcadero**.

2311   quay

la reina

2312   queen

hacer **una pregunta**

2313   to ask a **question**

¡Vuelve **rápido**!

2314   quick

Las arenas movedizas son muy peligrosas.

2315   quicksand

Ella es muy **tranquila**.

2316   She is **quiet**.

La pluma es más fuerte que la espada.

2317   quill

Los puercoespines tienen **púas**.

2318   porcupine **quill**

la colcha

2319   quilt/eiderdown*

Los niños llevan **membrillos** al colegio.

2320   quince

El carcaj sirve para llevar las flechas.

2321   quiver

temblar, estremecerse

2322   to quiver

la prueba

Hoy tuvimos **prueba** de ortografía en la escuela.

Our class had a quiz in spelling today.

2323   quiz

R

el conejo

2324   rabbit

el mapache, el oso lavador

2325   raccoon

echar carrera

2326   to race

la percha

2327   rack/hat-stand*

el alboroto, la baraúnda

2328   racket

el radiador

2329   radiator

la radio

2330   radio

los rábanos

2331   radish

¿Sabes sacar **el radio** del círculo?

2332   radius

la balsa

2333   raft

una invasión de hormigas

2334   a **raid** in progress

La baranda sirve para afirmarse.

2335   hand**rail**/banister*

la vía férrea

2336   railroad track/railway track*

¡Está **lloviendo** a chuzos!

2337   to rain

A todos los niños les gustan **los arco iris**.

2338   rainbow

el impermeable

2339   raincoat

levantar, plantear

¡Todos los que quieren a Marisol, que **levanten** la mano!
La pregunta que ella **plantea** es bastante interesante.

*All those who like Marisol, raise your hands!
She has raised an interesting question.*

2340   to **raise**

Las pasas son uvas secas.

2341   raisin

el rastrillo

2342   rake

El cartero **golpea** dos veces.	**rápido, veloz, raudo**	**raro, excepcional**	**el sarpullido**
2343 to rap/knock*	2344 rapid	2345 rare	2346 rash
las frambuesas	**la rata**	**el cascabel, el sonajero**	**la serpiente cascabel**
2347 raspberry	2348 rat	2349 rattle	2350 rattlesnake
el cuervo	**famélico, voraz**	**el barranco, la hondonada**	un huevo **crudo**
2351 raven	2352 ravenous	2353 ravine	2354 a raw egg
el rayo de luz	**la navaja de afeitar**	**alcanzar**	**leer**
2355 ray of sunlight	2356 razor	2357 to reach	2358 to read
Prepararse . . . **listo** . . .¡Ya!	¿Será **verdadero** este diamante?	**darse cuenta**	**¿De veras** que has llegado?
2359 ready	2360 real	2361 to realize/realise*	2362 Are you **really** here?

el trasero
2363   rear

el retrovisor
2364   rearview mirror

razonar, discutir, argüir
2365   to reason

módico, razonable
Este es un precio bastante **módico**.
¡Marisol, por favor, sé más **razonable**!

*That is a reasonable price.
Marisol, please be reasonable.*

2366   reasonable

rebelarse
La gente **se rebela** contra los altos impuestos.
Espartaco **se rebeló** contra Roma.

*People do rebel against high taxes.
Spartacus rebelled against Rome.*

2367   to rebel

No me puedo acordar.
2368   I do not recall.

recibir
2369   to receive

un pollito recién nacido
2370   recently hatched

la receta
2371   recipe

Y ahora les voy a recitar una poesía . . .
2372   to recite

el disco
2373   record

el tocadiscos
2374   record player

recuperarse, recobrar
Marisol se raspó la rodilla pero ya **se recuperó**.
Logré **recobrar** todos los libros que se quedaron afuera.

*Marisol scraped her knee but she's already recovered.
I recovered all the books that were left outside.*

2375   to recover

el rectángulo
2376   rectangle

el color rojo
2377   red

la caña, el junco
2378   reed

el arrecife de coral
2379   reef

¡Esa alcantarilla apesta!
2380   to reek

Las cañas de pescar tienen un carrete.
2381   reel

el árbitro
2382   referee

Las imágenes de un espejo se llaman **reflejos**.

2383   reflection

Siempre deja bien cerrado **el refrigerador**.

2384   refrigerator

rechazar, rehusar

2385   to refuse

una región

2386   region

inscribir, inscribirse

2387   to register

El pobre Martín **lamenta** mucho lo que pasó.

2388   to regret

Los actores **ensayan** una obra.

2389   Actors **rehearse** a play.

el reno

2390   reindeer

las riendas

2391   reins

los parientes, los familiares

2392   relatives

descansar, reposar

2393   to relax

soltar, liberar, poner en libertad

2394   to release

Acuérdate de lavarte los dientes.

2395   **Remember** to brush your teeth.

una isla muy **remota**

2396   **remote** island

quitar, sacar

2397   to remove

alquilar, arrendar

Nosotros **alquilamos** un departamento.
Si no tienes auto, podrías **arrendar** uno.

We rent an apartment.
If you do not have a car,
you can rent one.

2398   to rent

arreglar, reparar

2399   to repair

Los loros **repiten** lo que tú les digas.

2400   to repeat

cambiar, reponer

2401   to replace

¿Me podrías **responder** una pregunta?

2402   to reply

el reptil
2403   reptile

Javier **rescató** al pobre gatito.
2404   to rescue

el tanque, el depósito
2405   reservoir

responsable
Marisol, tú eres **responsable** de tu hermanito Raúl.
Papá vio la leche derramada en el suelo y dijo: "¿Quién es el **responsable** de esto?"

Marisol, you are responsible for your little brother Raul.
Dad saw the milk spilled on the floor and said: "Who is responsible for this?"

2406   responsible

descansar
2407   to rest

el restaurante, el restorán
2408   restaurant

devolver, volver
Marisol siempre **devuelve** los libros que saca de la biblioteca.
Gabriel anda de viaje pero **volverá** pronto.

Marisol always returns her library books.
Gabriel is travelling but he will return soon.

2409   to return

la marcha atrás
2410   reverse

el rinoceronte
2411   rhinoceros

el ruibarbo
2412   rhubarb

la rima
Este es un verso con **rima**:
Soy chiquitito
como una pepita de ají
pero tengo el corazón grande
para quererte a ti.

2413   rhyme

¿Será ésta **la costilla** de Adán?
2414   rib

un paquete adornado con **cinta** para regalo
2415   ribbon

El arroz es muy rico y nutritivo.
2416   rice

intenso, rico
Este género es de un rojo **intenso**.
Ese es un colegio para **ricos**.

The fabric is a rich red color.
That's a school for the rich.

2417   rich

¡Vaya qué **misterio**!
2418   riddle

montar, cabalgar
2419   to ride a horse

el cerro, el reborde
2420   ridge

Esta es mi mano **derecha**.
2421   my right hand

la derecha, bien, cierto
Al llegar a la esquina dobla a **la derecha**.
No está **bien** robar.
Marisol cree que siempre está en lo **cierto**.

Turn right at the corner.
It is not right to steal.
Marisol thinks she is always right.

2422   right

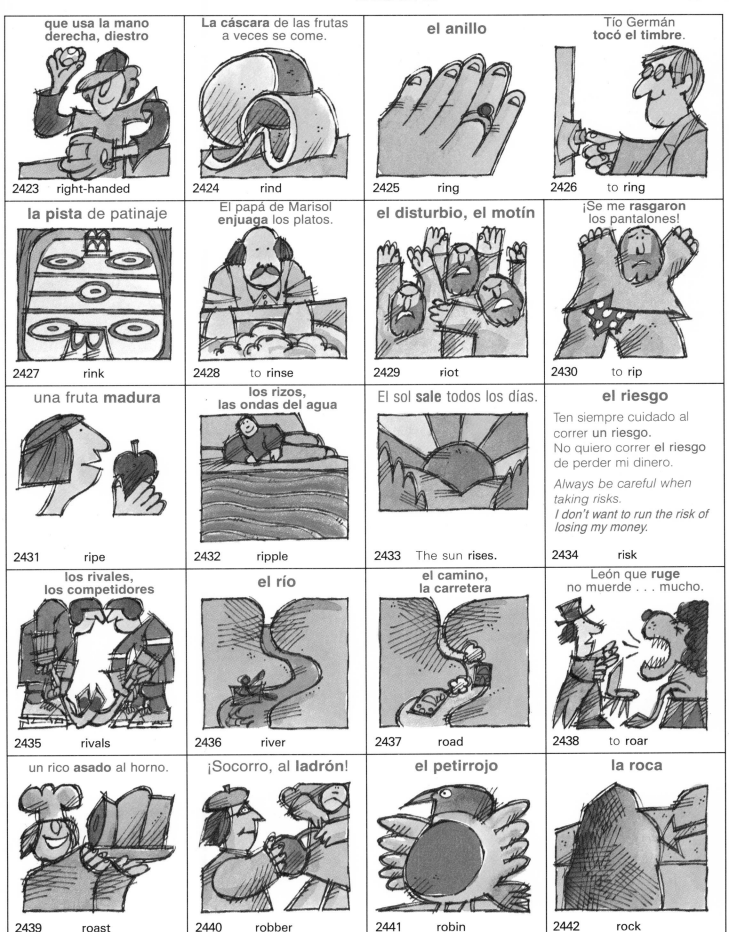

que usa la mano derecha, diestro

2423   right-handed

La cáscara de las frutas a veces se come.

2424   rind

el anillo

2425   ring

Tío Germán **tocó el timbre**.

2426   to ring

la pista de patinaje

2427   rink

El papá de Marisol **enjuaga** los platos.

2428   to rinse

el disturbio, el motín

2429   riot

¡Se me **rasgaron** los pantalones!

2430   to rip

una fruta **madura**

2431   ripe

los rizos, las ondas del agua

2432   ripple

El sol **sale** todos los días.

2433   The sun **rises**.

el riesgo

Ten siempre cuidado al correr **un riesgo**.
No quiero correr **el riesgo** de perder mi dinero.

Always be careful when taking risks.
I don't want to run the risk of losing my money.

2434   risk

los rivales, los competidores

2435   rivals

el río

2436   river

el camino, la carretera

2437   road

León que **ruge** no muerde . . . mucho.

2438   to roar

un rico **asado** al horno.

2439   roast

¡Socorro, al **ladrón**!

2440   robber

el petirrojo

2441   robin

la roca

2442   rock

balancearse, mecerse 2443 to rock	**el cohete** 2444 rocket	**la mecedora** 2445 rocking chair	**la caña** de pescar 2446 rod
el rollo de papel 2447 roll	**rodar** 2448 to roll	los **patines de ruedas** 2449 roller skate	**el uslero, el rodillo** 2450 rolling pin
el techo de la casa 2451 roof	**el cuarto, la sala, la habitación** 2452 room	descansar las aves en una percha 2453 to roost	**la raíz** 2454 root
la soga, la cuerda 2455 rope	**la rosa** 2456 rose	**el romero** 2457 rosemary	María Paz tiene las mejillas **rosadas**. 2458 rosy
una manzana **podrida** 2459 rotten apple	una barba **áspera** 2460 rough	**redondo** 2461 round	cuatro botones en **fila** 2462 4 buttons in a row

Lucía **rema** más rápido que su hermano.

2463 to row

El rey es el jefe de la casa **real**.

2464 royal

Los neumáticos y las pelotas se hacen de **caucho**.

2465 rubber

la basura, los desechos

2466 rubbish

el rubí

2467 ruby

el timón

2468 rudder

un tipo **grosero**

2469 He is rude.

un territorio **escarpado, escabroso**

2470 rugged terrain

Estas son **las ruinas** de un antiguo castillo.

2471 ruin

la regla

La excepción confirma la regla.
Tú conoces las reglas del juego.

The exception confirms the rule.
You know the rules of the game.

2472 rule

Este es **un gobernante** antiguo.

2473 ruler

Se oye **el retumbo** de un tren.

2474 I hear a rumble.

Nunca **corras** al cruzar la calle.

2475 to run

huir, escaparse

2476 to run away

atropellar

2477 to run over

agotarse

2478 to run out of energy

apurarse, apresurarse, darse prisa

2479 to rush

el óxido

2480 rust

el bache, la rodada

2481 rut

Me gusta el pan **centeno**.

2482 rye

el saco de harina

2483   sack

Decir la verdad es un precepto **sagrado**.

2484   Truth is a **sacred** principle.

triste

2485   sad

la montura

2486   saddle

¿Qué hay en **la caja fuerte**?

2487   safe

la vela de una carabela

2488   sail

la tabla, la plancha a vela

2489   sailboard

el velero

2490   sailboat/sailing boat*

el marino, el marinero

2491   sailor

la ensalada

2492   salad

a precios de **liquidación**

2493   sale

el salmón

2494   salmon

la sal y la pimienta

2495   salt

saludar, hacer un saludo

2496   to salute

igual, lo **mismo**

2497   same

un reloj de **arena**

2498   sand

la sandalia

2499   sandal

De almuerzo me comí **un sandwich**.

2500   sandwich

la savia

2501   sap

como **sardinas** en lata

2502   sardine

el satélite

2503   satellite

un vestido de **raso**

2504   satin dress

el sábado

El sábado es el sexto día de la semana.
Los sábados se juega y nada más.
A Marisol le encantan los **sábados**.

Saturday is the sixth day of the week.
Saturday is play day.
Marisol likes Saturdays.

2505   Saturday

la salsa

2506   sauce/gravy*

la salchicha

2507   sausage

Yo **ahorro** dinero.

2508   I save my money.

El serrucho es una herramienta muy útil.

2509   saw

Aserrín, aserrán, los maderos de San Juan . . .

2511   sawdust

Yo **digo** las cosas tal como son.

2512   I say what I think.

el andamiaje

2513   scaffolding

aserruchar, aserrar, serrar

2510   to saw

quemarse con agua hirviendo, escaldarse

2514   to scald

El fiel de **la balanza** controla el peso.

2515   scale

¡**Los ostiones** son cosa muy rica, señor!

2516   scallop

el cuero cabelludo

2517   scalp

una cicatriz en la cara y otra en el corazón

2518   scar

A Martín le revienta que lo **asusten**.

2519   to scare

Los espantapájaros no tienen cerebro.

2520   scarecrow

la bufanda

2521   scarf

el color **escarlata**
2522 scarlet

El criminal vuelve a **la escena** del crimen.
2523 scene of a crime

el paisaje
2524 scenery

El saber no ocupa lugar.
2525 scholarship

Esta es **la escuela** de Marisol.
2526 school

la goleta
2527 schooner

las tijeras
2528 scissors

sacar con cuchara o pala
2529 to scoop

la motoneta
2530 scooter

un papel **chamuscado**
2531 scorched paper

marcar un tanto, meter un gol
2532 to score

un niño explorador
2533 scout

unos pedazos de papel
2534 scraps of paper

¡Otra **raspadura**!
2535 scrape

el raspador
2536 scraper

el rasguño
2537 scratch

la rejilla
2538 screen

el tornillo
2539 screw

el atornillador, el destornillador
2540 screwdriver

Mamá trabaja **fregando** pisos.
2541 to scrub

el escultor	**el caballito de mar, el hipocampo**	**El Mar** Adriático está cerca del **Mar** Jónico.	**la gaviota**
2542　sculptor	2543　seahorse	2544　Adriatic sea	2545　seagull
la foca	**una costura**	**buscar, explorar**	**el reflector**
2546　seal	2547　seam	2548　to search	2549　searchlight
la estación Las cuatro **estaciones** son: primavera verano otoño invierno *The four seasons are: Spring Summer Autumn Winter*	**el asiento**	Marisol siempre se pone **el cinturón de seguridad**.	**las algas**
2550　seasons	2551　seat	2552　seatbelt	2553　seaweed
Llegó **segundo**.	Tengo **un secreto**.	**ver**	**el balancín, el sube y baja**
2554　second	2555　I have a **secret**.	2556　to see	2557　see-saw
la semilla	**Parece** que se murió . . .	**agarrar, coger**	A nadie le gustan las personas **egoístas**.
2558　seed	2559　It **seems** to be dead.	2560　to seize	2561　You are **selfish**.

Iris **vende** frutas.

2562   to **sell**

el **semicírculo**

2563   semicircle

enviar, despachar, remitir

2564   to **send**

La tarde al sol me dejó la piel **sensible**.

2565   **sensitive** skin

la frase, la sentencia

¿Tú podrías escribir una frase?
Al ladrón le dieron una larga **sentencia**.

Can you make a sentence?
The robber received a long prison sentence.

2566   sentence

el **centinela**

2567   sentry

Septiembre es el noveno mes del año.

2568   September

servir

2569   to **serve**

el número **siete**

2570   seven

séptimo

2571   seventh

varios

2572   several

coser y cantar

2573   to **sew**

la **máquina de coser**

2574   sewing machine

andrajoso, harapiento

2575   shabby

la **choza**

2576   shack

la **sombra**

2577   shadow

un perro **lanudo**

2578   shaggy

sacudir, agitar

2579   to **shake**

agua **poco profunda**

2580   shallow water

Mamá se lava el pelo con **champú**.

2581   shampoo

Yo **comparto** lo que tengo con los demás.

2582   to share

Los tiburones no tienen huesos en el cuerpo.

2583   shark

afilado

2584   sharp

el afilador de cuchillos

2585   knife sharpener

El vaso **se hizo añicos**.

2588   to shatter

afeitar, rasurarse

2589   to shave

las cizallas, las tijeras de podar

2590   shears

el afilador de patines

2586   skate sharpener

la funda

2591   sheath

Marisol cuenta **ovejas** para quedarse dormida.

2592   sheep

la sábana

2593   sheet

el sacapuntas

2587   pencil sharpener

el estante, la repisa

2594   shelf

la concha

2595   shell

a buen **resguardo**

2596   shelter

el pastor

2597   shepherd

el escudo

2598   shield

la canilla

2599   shin

El sol **brilla** esplendoroso.

2600   to shine

Los tejados tienen **tejas**.

2601   shingle

La zona es una enfermedad cutánea.

2602   shingles

brillante, resplandeciente

2603   shiny

la embarcación, la nave

2604   ship

el naufragio

2605   shipwreck

la camisa

2606   shirt

tiritar, temblar

2607   to shiver

¡Cuidado con **los golpes eléctricos!**

2608   shock

los zapatos

2609   shoes

los cordones, los pasadores

2610   shoelace

el zapatero

2611   shoemaker

disparar, tirar

2612   to shoot

la tienda, el almacén

2613   shop

el almacenero, el tendero

2614   shopkeeper

la vitrina, el escaparate

2615   shop window

a **orillas** del mar

2616   shore

bajo

2617   short

los pantalones cortos, los shorts

2618   shorts

el hombro

2619   shoulder

gritar

2620   to shout

Empujar a alguien es pésima educación.

2621   to shove

la pala

2622   shovel

mostrar, enseñar

2623   to show

alardear, vanagloriarse, hacer ostentación

2624   to show off

Por fin apareció.

2625   to show up/appear*

Ricardo canta en **la ducha.**

2626   shower

chillar, dar alaridos

2627   to shriek

el camarón, la gamba

2628   shrimp

encoger, encogerse

2629   to shrink

el arbusto

2630   shrub

Así se **baraja** la baraja.

2631   shuffle

los postigos, las contraventanas

2632   shutters

tímido, vergonzoso

2633   shy

enfermo

2634   sick

el lado, el costado

2635   side

Siempre es mejor caminar por **la vereda.**

2636   sidewalk/pavement*

al salir del examen **suspiré** de alivio

2637   to sigh

el letrero, el cartel

2638   sign

indicar, señalar

2639   to signal

mi **firma**

2640   signature

callado, silencioso

Marisol nunca se está **callada** mucho rato.
Una noche **silenciosa** es una noche tranquila.

Marisol is not silent very often.
A silent night is a quiet night.

2641   silent

el pretil de la ventana

2642 sill

tonto, necio

Manolito dice que Marisol es **tonta**.
Marisol piensa que el **necio** es Manolito.

Manolito thinks Marisol is silly.
Marisol thinks Manolito is the silly one.

2643 silly

la plata

2644 silver

simple, sencillo

Esa es la pura y **simple** verdad.
Esto tiene una solución muy **sencilla**.

That is the truth, pure and simple.
There is a simple solution.

2645 simple

cantar

2646 to sing

singular

Plural es lo contrario de **singular**.
"Uno" es **singular**.

Plural is the opposite of singular.
"One is singular.

2647 singular

el lavatorio, el lavamanos, el lavabo

2648 sink

¡Nos hundimos!

2649 to sink

Alejandra **sorbe** su trago con fruición.

2650 to sip

Esta **sirena** no sabe nadar.

2651 siren

Esta es mi **hermana** Lili.

2652 sister

tomar asiento, sentarse

2653 to sit

seis

2654 six

sexto

2655 sixth

¿Será de mi **talla**?

2656 size

patinar

2657 to skate

el monopatín

2658 skateboard

¡Ojalá tuviéramos **un esqueleto** de repuesto!

2659 skeleton

hacer un boceto, un croquis, un bosquejo

2660 to sketch

los esquíes

2661 skis

esquiar
2662   to ski

resbalarse, patinar
2663   to skid

la piel
2664   skin

saltar la cuerda
2665   to skip

el capitán, el patrón del barco
2666   skipper / captain*

la falda
2667   skirt

el cráneo, una calavera
2668   skull

el cielo
2669   sky

la alondra, la calandria
2670   skylark

Un rascacielos es un edificio muy alto.
2671   skyscraper

Raúl cerró de un portazo.
2672   to slam

un piso inclinado
2673   slanting floor

abofetear, dar una palmada
2674   to slap

El Zorro da tajos a destajo.
2675   to slash

la pizarra
2676   slate

el trineo
2677   sled / sleigh*

De día, Zorro duerme.
2678   to sleep

el saco de dormir
2679   sleeping bag

Jorge tiene sueño.
2680   sleepy

la cellisca
2681   sleet

la manga

2682   sleeve

el resbalín, el tobogán

2683   slide

delgada, flaca

2684   slim

un bicho viscoso

2685   slimy

con el brazo en cabestrillo

2686   sling

la honda, el tirador

2687   slingshot / catapult*

resbalar, resbalarse

2688   to slip

la zapatilla, la pantufla

2689   slipper

resbaloso

2690   slippery

un tipo mugriento y ordinario

2691   slob

la ladera

2692   slope

la ranura

2693   slot

No andes tan desgarbado.

2694   to slouch

disminuir la velocidad, ir más despacio, parar

El auto **disminuyó la velocidad** al llegar a la esquina.
¡Más despacio, papá! Estás yendo muy rápido.
A Marisol no la **para** nadie.

The car slows down at the corner.
Slow down, Dad! You are going too fast.
Nothing can slow down Marisol.

2695   to slow down

el aguanieve

2696   slush

pequeño

2697   small

listo, sensato, elegante

Marisol se cree muy **lista** porque le fue bien en el examen.
Lo que hiciste fue muy **sensato**.
El vestido que lleva es muy **elegante**.

Marisol thinks she is very smart because she passed her exam.
That was a smart thing to do.
She is wearing a smart dress.

2698   smart / clever*

¡No hagas pedazos el reloj!

2699   to smash

manchar, embadurnar, hacer un borrón

2700   to smear

A Luis le gusta oler las flores.

2701   to smell

¡Qué zorrillo más hediondo!

2702   smelly

Los que fuman son como zorrillos.

2703   to smoke

suave, parejo

La seda es una tela muy **suave**.
Este camino es muy **parejo**.

Silk is a very smooth fabric.
This is a very smooth road.

2704   smooth

comerse un tentempié

2705   to have a snack

Caracol, caracol, saca tus cachitos al sol.

2706   snail

una culebra, una serpiente

2707   snake

partirse en dos, romperse

2708   to snap

las zapatillas

2709   sneakers/trainers*

estornudar

2710   to sneeze

el tubo respiratorio, el snorkel

2711   snorkel

la nieve

2712   snow

el copo de nieve

2713   snowflake

las raquetas de nieve

2714   snowshoes

Lávate con agua y **jabón**.

2715   soap

el fútbol, pasión de multitudes

2716   soccer

el calcetín

2717   sock

el enchufe, el tomacorriente

2718   socket

el sofá

2719   sofa/couch*

Suave será, pero igual araña.

2720   soft

el soldado

2721   soldier

Los lenguados son muy deslenguados.

2722   sole

Resolvió el problema.

2723   She **solves** the problem.

dar un salto mortal

2724   to **somersault**

Este es mi **hijo**.

2725   son

el canto, la canción

2726   song

dentro de poco, luego, al poco rato

Va a oscurecer **dentro de poco**.
Marisol vuelve **luego**.
Al poco rato se cansó de la muñeca nueva.

Soon it will be dark.
Marisol will be home soon.
She soon tired of her new doll.

2727   soon

el hechicero, el brujo

2728   sorcerer

Tengo el brazo **adolorido**.

2729   My arm is **sore**.

La acedera es muy sabrosa.

2730   sorrel

Macabeo está muy **arrepentido** de lo que hizo.

2731   sorry

separar, escoger, seleccionar

2732   to **sort**

¿Qué odiaba Mafalda? ¡**La sopa**!

2733   soup

agrio, ácido

2734   sour

rumbo al **sur**

2735   south

una cerda, chancha, puerca, marrana, cochina

2736   sow

sembrar

2737   to sow

la nave espacial

2738   spaceship

la pala

2739   spade

zurrar

2740   to spank

Siempre conviene tener un neumático de **repuesto**.

2741   spare tire/tyre*

la chispa

2742   spark

Los anillos **relumbran** a la luz.

2743   to sparkle

el gorrión

2744   sparrow

¿Cuántos idiomas sabes **hablar**?

2745   to speak

una lanza

2746   spear

La tortuga va a paso de tortuga incluso cuando **acelera**.

2747   to speed up

deletrear

2748   to spell

gastar

2749   to spend

Las esferas son redondas.

2750   sphere

picante y **condimentado**

2751   spicy

Las arañas no arañan.

2752   spider

la punta, la púa

2753   spike

derramar, desparramar

2754   to spill

girar, dar vueltas

2755   to spin

la espinaca

2756   spinach

la espina dorsal

2757   spine

la espiral

2758   spiral

la aguja de una iglesia

2759   spire

Las personas bien educadas no **escupen**.

2760   to spit

salpicar

2761   to splash

Saltan **astillas** por todos lados.	la fruta **podrida**	**la esponja**	**el carrete** o **la bobina** de hilo
2762 splinter	2763 spoiled/rotten* fruit	2764 sponge	2765 spool/reel*
la cuchara	¿Y de dónde salió esta **mancha**?	**el pico** de la tetera	Marisol **se torció** un tobillo.
2766 spoon	2767 spot	2768 spout	2769 to sprain
rociar	**esparcir**	**el resorte, el muelle**	¡Al fin llegó **la primavera**!
2770 to spray	2771 to spread	2772 spring	2773 spring
espolvorear	**correr a gran velocidad**	**el abeto**	**El manantial** trae agua fría y fresca.
2775 to sprinkle	2776 to sprint	2777 spruce	2774 spring
un cuadrado	**la calabaza, el calabacín**	**ponerse en cuclillas**	Marisol **estrechó** a Rosita en sus brazos.
2778 square	2779 squash	2780 to squat	2781 to squeeze

el calamar

2782 squid

la ardilla

2783 squirrel

chorrear, salir a chorros

2784 to squirt

Los caballos viven en **los establos**.

2785 stable

el escenario del teatro

2786 stage

la mancha

2787 stain

la escalera

2788 staircase

una estaca de madera

2789 wooden stake

añejo

El pan **añejo** se pone duro y seco.

Stale bread is dry and hard.

2790 stale bread

un tallo de apio

2791 celery stalk

Un potro es un caballo macho.

2792 stallion

la estampilla, el sello

2793 stamp

pararse, estar de pie

2794 to stand

Las estrellas son rayos de luz vieja.

2795 star

Marisol te **mira fijamente**.

2796 to stare

el estornino

2797 starling

poner en marcha un coche

2798 to start a car

estar famélico, morir de hambre

Cuando Marisol dice ''estoy **famélica**'', quiere decir que tiene hambre.
¡No te vas a **morir de hambre**, Marisol!

When Marisol says ''I'm starving'', she means that she is hungry.
You will not starve, Marisol!

2799 to starve

la bencinera, la estación de servicio, **la gasolinera**

2800 gas/petrol* station

la estación de trenes

2801 train/railway* station

la estatua

2802　statue

¡Quédate ahí!

2803　Stay there!

el bistec

2804　steak

robar

2805　to steal

el vapor

2806　steam

Los cuchillos se hacen de **acero**.

2807　Kinves are made of steel.

empinado

2808　steep

la res, el novillo

2809　steer/bullock*

el tallo

2811　stem

el escalón, el peldaño, la grada

2812　step

¡Me metí en un charco!

2813　to step in

guiar, conducir, dirigir

2810　to steer

Papá preparó **un estofado** para la comida.

2815　stew

el palo, la vara

2816　stick

Voy a **salir** un ratito.

2814　to step out

Vicente tiene las manos **pegajosas**.

2817　sticky

duro, tieso

Malandrín el ladrón recibió una **dura** condena.
Amanecí con el cuello **tieso**.

Malandrin the thief received a stiff sentence.
I got up with a stiff neck.

2818　stiff

La picadura me **escuece** y me **duele.**

2819　to sting

la picadura de abeja

2820　sting

Los zorrillos **apestan**.

2821　to stink

Revuelve bien antes de tomártelo.

2822 to **stir**

las **medias**

2823 **stockings**

atizar

2824 to **stoke**

el **estómago**

2825 **stomach**

Los picapedreros pican **piedras**.

2826 **stone**

el taburete, la banqueta, el piso

2827 **stool**

Yo **me agacho** a recoger la pelota.

2828 to **stoop/bend down***

el alto, la parada

2829 **stop**

la tienda, el almacén

2832 **store/shop***

¿Quién trae a los niños? **¿La cigüeña?**

2833 **stork**

la tormenta, la tempestad

2834 **storm**

El Supertipo **detuvo** el tren.

2830 He **stops** the train.

La Tía María nos leyó **un cuento**.

2835 **story**

la **cocina**

2836 **stove/cooker***

derecho, recto

2837 **straight**

una **escala** técnica

2831 to **stop over**

colar

2838 to **strain**

esforzarse

2839 to **strain**

un animalejo muy **raro**

2840 **strange**

¡Quique se acercó mucho y el gorila lo va a **estrangular**!

2841 to **strangle**

el tirante

2842   strap

la paja, la pajilla

2843   straw

la frutilla, la fresa

2844   strawberry

el arroyo

2845   stream

el banderín, el gallardete

2846   streamer/pennant*

la calle

2847   street

el farol

2848   street light/lamp*

¿Hasta dónde se podrá **estirar**?

2849   to stretch

la camilla

2850   stretcher

la huelga

Los obreros están en **huelga** por mejores salarios.

The workers are on strike for more money.

2851   strike

No es bueno **golpear** a otra persona.

2852   to strike

la cuerda, el cordel

2853   string

un género a **rayas**

2854   stripe

fuerte

2855   strong

el alumno, el estudiante

2856   student

estudiar

2857   to study

un **animalito de juguete**

2858   a **stuffed** animal

el tocón

2859   stump

Yo prefiero **el submarino** amarillo.

2860   submarine

restar

2861   to subtract

chupar	**de repente, precipitadamente**	Comer mucha **azúcar** no hace bien.	**el terno, el traje**
2862 to suck	**De repente** se puso a llover. Gabriela se fue **precipitadamente**. *Suddenly, it began to rain.* *Gabriela left suddenly.* 2863 suddenly	2864 sugar	2865 suit
la maleta, la valija	¡Qué lindo es **el verano**!	**el sol**	**el domingo**
2866 suitcase	2867 summer	2868 sun	**El domingo** es el séptimo día de la semana. *Sunday is the seventh day of the week.* 2869 Sunday
Un reloj de sol no se atrasa.	**El girasol** gira con el sol.	**la salida del sol**	**la puesta del sol**
2870 sundial	2871 sunflower	2872 sunrise	2873 sunset
¿Me acompañas al **supermercado**?	**la cena, la comida**	**seguro**	**la superficie** lunar
2874 supermarket	2875 supper/dinner*	Estoy **seguro** de que mañana será un día soleado. **Seguro** que Marisol va mañana. *I am sure tomorrow will be a sunny day.* *Marisol will go tomorrow for sure.* 2876 sure	2877 surface
el cirujano	**el apellido**	una fiesta de **sorpresa**	**rendirse**
2878 surgeon	Mi nombre es Marisol y mi **apellido** es Martínez. *My first name is Marisol and my surname is Martinez.* 2879 surname	2880 surprise party	2881 to surrender

Estos tipos me tienen **rodeado**.

2882   to **surround**

los suspensores, los tirantes

2883   suspenders/braces*

tragar

2884   to **swallow**

el cisne

2885   swan

permutar, trocar, intercambiar

2886   to **swap**

¡Un enjambre de abejas asesinas!

2887   swarm

sudar, transpirar

2888   to **sweat**

el suéter, la chompa, la chomba

2889   sweater/sweatshirt*

barrer

2890   to **sweep**

dulce

2891   sweet

Tuvimos que **virar bruscamente** a causa de ese gato.

2892   to **swerve**

nadar

2893   to **swim**

el columpio

2894   swing

columpiarse

2895   to **swing**

el interruptor

2896   switch

encender, cambiar, apagar

Enciende las luces, por favor.
Si quieres te **cambio** el asiento y así ves mejor.
Lo mejor es **apagar** el televisor.

Switch on the light, please.
Shall we switch seats so you can see better?
It is best to switch off the television.

2897   to **switch**

abalanzarse, abatirse sobre algo

2898   to **swoop**

la espada

2899   sword

el sicómoro, el sicomoro

2900   sycamore

¿Te gustan los panqueques con **jarabe**?

2901   syrup

la mesa

2902　table

el mantel

2903　tablecloth

la tableta

2904　tablet

una tachuela

2905　tack

abordar, atajar

Marisol tendrá que **abordar** pronto el problema.
¿Viste cómo Alfredo **atajó** a Guillermo durante el partido de fútbol?

Marisol must tackle that problem soon.
Did you see how Alfredo tackled Guillermo during the football game?

2906　to **tackle**

Los renacuajos se convierten en ranas.

2907　tadpole

la cola, el rabo

2908　tail

tomar, coger, asir

2910　to **take**

desarmar

2911　to **take apart**

llevar, llevarse

2912　to **take away**

devolver, llevar de vuelta

2913　to **take back**

quitarse, sacarse

2914　to **take off**

despegar

2915　to **take off**

sacar, extraer

2916　to **take out**

Compré comida **para llevar.**

2917　take-out / take-away*

el sastre

2909　tailor

el cuento, el chisme, el relato

2918　tale

el talento

Lucía y Marisol demonstraron ser cantantes **de talento.**
Marta tiene mucho **talento** para el teatro.

Lucia and Marisol showed themselves to be talented singers.
Marta has a great talent for acting.

2919　talent

hablar

2920　to **talk**

alto, espigado

2921   tall

el pandero, la pandereta

2922   tambourine

Los leones circenses son bastante **mansos**.

2923   tame

¡Qué hermoso **bronceado**!

2924   tan

la mandarina

2925   tangerine

enredado, enmarañado

2926   tangled

el tanque, el depósito

2927   tank

el buque tanque, el buque cisterna

2928   tanker

Esta **llave** está goteando.

2929   tap

un rollo de **cinta**

2930   tape

pegar, fijar con cinta adhesiva

2931   to tape

la grabadora, el grabador

2932   tape recorder

la brea, el alquitrán

2933   tar

La flecha dio en **el blanco**.

2934   target

El estragón se usa en las comidas.

2935   tarragon

la tarta, el pastel de frutas

2936   tart

Mi **tarea** es barrer el piso.

2937   task

probar, paladear, saborear, degustar

2938   to taste

sabroso

Esta comida está muy sabrosa.

This is very tasty food.

2939   tasty

el taxi, el coche de alquiler

2940   taxi

una tacita de **té**

2941   a cup of **tea**

La Sra. González nos **enseña** matemáticas.

2942   to **teach**

Ella es **la profesora** de mi curso.

2943   **teacher**

Yo juego en **el equipo** de béisbol.

2944   **team**

la tetera

2945   **teapot**

la lágrima

2946   **tear**

rasgar, romper, desgarrar

2947   to **tear**

Nunca **arranques** las páginas de un libro.

2948   to **tear out**

el telegrama

2949   **telegram**

el teléfono

2950   **telephone**

llamar por teléfono, telefonear

2951   to **telephone**

el telescopio

2952   **telescope**

La tele es lo mismo que **la televisión**.

2953   **television**

decir, contar, narrar, relatar

2954   to **tell**

el genio, el mal humor

Macabeo tiene mal **genio**. A veces no puede controlar su **mal humor**.

Macabeo has a bad temper.
He cannot control his temper.

2955   **temper**

la temperatura

2956   **temperature**

diez manzanitas

2957   **ten** apples

raqueta y pelota de **tenis**

2958   **tennis** racquet and ball

una zapatilla de **tenis**

2959   **tennis** shoe

Anoche Marisol durmió en una **tienda de campaña**.

2960   **tent**

décimo	**un terminal** de computación	**probar** el agua	**agradecer, dar las gracias**
2961 tenth	2962 terminal	2963 to **test** the water	2964 to **thank**
Al llegar la primavera el suelo **se deshiela**.	**el teatro**	**allí, ahí, allá**	**el termómetro**
2965 to **thaw**	2966 theater/theatre*	2967 there	2968 thermometer
tupido, grueso, denso, espeso	**Ladrón** que roba a **ladrón** . . .	**el muslo**	**el dedal**
2969 thick	2970 thief	2971 thigh	2972 thimble
ralo, flaco, delgado	**la cosa** Una persona no es una **cosa**. Marisol dice **cosas** muy graciosas. *A person is not a thing. Marisol says many funny things.*	**pensar**	**tercero**
2973 thin	2974 thing	2975 to **think**	2976 third
sediento	**un cardo** burrero	**Las espinas** pinchan.	**el hilo**
2977 thirsty	2978 thistle	2979 thorn	2980 thread

Marisol sabe **enhebrar** agujas.

2981   to thread

tres

2982   three

el umbral

2983   threshold

la garganta

2984   throat

Este es **el trono** del rey.

2985   throne

tirar, lanzar, arrojar

2986   to throw

vomitar

2987   to throw up/be sick*

el dedo **pulgar**

2988   thumb

Caían rayos y **truenos**.

2989   thunder

la tormenta eléctrica, la tronada

2990   thunderstorm

el jueves

El jueves es el cuarto día de la semana.
Marisol acude a clases de natación **los jueves**.

Thursday is the fourth day of the week.
Marisol goes to swimming class on Thursdays.

2991   Thursday

con **tomillo** y laurel

2992   thyme

el billete, el boleto, la entrada, el pasaje

2993   ticket

cosquillear, hacer cosquillas

2994   to tickle

Al menos uno de los dos se ve **aseado**.

2995   tidy

¿Sabes hacer un nudo de **corbata**?

2996   tie

el tigre de Malasia

2998   tiger

apretar, estrechar

2999   to tighten

las losas, las baldosas, los azulejos

3000   tiles

atar, amarrar, liar

2997   to tie

¡El bote se está **ladeando**!	**¿Qué hora es?**	**diminuto, menudo**	El bote terminó por **volcarse**.
3001 to **tilt**	3002 What **time** is it?	3003 tiny	3004 to **tip**
caminar de puntillas	El coche necesita **llantas** nuevas.	**cansado, fatigado**	**dar propina**
3006 tiptoe	3007 tire/tyre*	3008 tired	3005 to **tip**
el sapo cancionero	**unas tostadas** con mantequilla	**la tostadora**	**hoy día, hoy** Las clases comienzan **hoy** día. **Hoy** es el Día de la Madre. ¡Haz tus deberes **hoy** mismo! *School starts today.* *Today is Mothers' Day.* *Do your homework today!*
3009 toad	3010 toast	3011 toaster	3012 today
los dedos del pie	Nosotros nos sentamos **juntos**.	**el inodoro, el retrete, el excusado**	**el tomate**
3013 toes	3014 We are sitting **together**.	3015 toilet	3016 tomato
la tumba, la sepultura	**mañana** **Mañana** será otro día. Marisol irá **mañana** al museo a ver los dinosaurios. *Tomorrow is another day.* *Marisol is going to see dinosaurs at the museum tomorrow.*	**las tenazas**	Yo no tengo pelos en **la lengua**.
3017 tomb	3018 tomorrow	3019 tongs	3020 tongue

¡Éste pesa **una tonelada**!	**las amígdalas**	**las herramientas**	**el diente**
3021 It weighs a **ton**.	3022 tonsils	3023 tools	3024 tooth

el dolor de muelas	el cepillo de dientes	la pasta de dientes	**la parte superior, la parte de arriba**
3025 toothache	3026 toothbrush	3027 toothpaste	3028 top

Las cajas **se vinieron abajo**.	**la antorcha** olímpica	**el tornado**	**El trompo** gira y gira.
3030 to topple	3031 torch	3032 tornado	3029 top

el torrente, el raudal	**la tortuga**	Martín **arrojó** la pelota a su amiguita.	**tocar**
3033 torrent	3034 tortoise	3035 to **toss**	3036 to touch

Yo soy un tipo **recio**.	**remolcar**	Marisol tiene **una toalla** favorita.	**la torre** más alta del mundo
3037 I am **tough**.	3038 to tow	3039 towel	3040 tower

Marisol vive en este **pueblo**.
3041 town

¡Recojan sus **juguetes**, niños!
3042 toys

calcar
3043 to trace

el riel, la vía férrea
3044 track

el tractor
3045 tractor

cambiar, trocar, canjear, permutar
3046 to trade

un embotellamiento de **tráfico**
3047 traffic

el semáforo
3048 traffic light

el rastro, la pista
3049 trail

el remolque para caballitos
3050 trailer

¿Te gusta viajar en **tren**?
3051 train

Macabeo está muy bien **amaestrado**.
3052 to train

el vagabundo
3053 tramp

¡No **pisoteen** las flores!
3054 to trample

el trampolín
3055 trampoline

Casi todos los vidrios son **transparentes**.
3056 transparent

transportar, acarrear
3057 to transport

el transportador
3058 transporter/lorry*

la trampa para ratones
3059 trap

Este es Martín, artista del **trapecio**.
3060 trapeze

Tía Carlina **viaja** con mucha frecuencia.

3061   to travel

Nos trajeron los tragos en **bandeja**.

3062   tray

las estrías de un neumático

3063   tread

el tesoro del filibustero

3064   treasure

el árbol

3065   tree

Yolanda quedó **temblando** de susto.

3066   to tremble

la zanja, el foso

3067   trench

el juicio, el proceso

3068   trial

Todos **los triángulos** tienen tres lados.

3069   triangle

truco de magia

3070   trick

El agua **chorrea** despacio.

3071   to trickle

el triciclo

3072   tricycle

Un gatillo no es un gato.

3073   trigger

recortar

3074   to trim

un viaje corto

3075   a short **trip**

tropezar, dar un traspié

3076   to trip

el trole, el trolebús

3077   trolley bus

A los potrillos les gusta **trotar**.

3078   to trot

el comedero de animales

3079   trough

los pantalones

3080   trousers

la trucha

3081   trout

la llana, la plana, la paleta

3082   trowel

el camión

3083   truck/lorry*

cierto, verdadero, verídico

¿Es **cierto** que Marisol cruzó el mar a nado?
¿**Verdadero** o falso?
¿Será ése un relato **verídico**?

Is it true that Marisol swam across the ocean?
True or false?
Is that a true story?

3084   true

la trompeta, la corneta

3085   trumpet

el baúl

3086   trunk

el tronco de un árbol

3087   trunk

la trompa de un elefante

3088   trunk

Confío en tu palabra.

3089   to trust

Me alegro de que hayas dicho la verdad.

3090   truth

tratar, poner a prueba, intentar

Trata de recordar dónde pones las cosas.
¡Marisol, no **pongas a prueba** mi paciencia!
Tienes que **intentar** otra vez.

Try to remember where you put your things.
Marisol, do not try my patience!
You must try again.

3091   to try

la tina, la bañera

3092   tub

el tubo, el caño

3093   tube

el martes

El martes es el segundo día de la semana.
Los martes Marisol tiene clases de piano.

Tuesday is the second day of the week.
On Tuesdays, Marisol has piano lessons.

3094   Tuesday

tirar de la cuerda

3095   to tug

Los tulipanes son flores de corta vida.

3096   tulip

dar volteretas, caer, dar tumbos, rodar

3097   to tumble

el túnel

3098   tunnel

un pavo plebeyo

3099   turkey

dar vuelta, girar

3100   to turn

apagar

3101　to turn off

encender

3102　to turn on

resultar, salir

Enrique **resultó** ser un mal muchacho.
Las cosas **salieron** bien.

Enrique turned out to be a bad boy.
Things turned out well.

3103　to turn out

Laura le **dio** una **vuelta** a la carne.

3104　to turn over

el nabo

3105　turnip

el plato giratorio

3106　turntable

el color turquesa

3107　turquoise

la torreta, la torrecilla

3108　turret

la tortuga

3109　turtle

Los colmillos son el colmo.

3110　tusk

las pinzas

3111　tweezers

dos veces, el doble

Marisol ha ido al zoológico **dos veces**.
Ricardo tiene **el doble** de libros que yo.

Marisol has been to the zoo twice.
Ricardo has twice as many books as I.

3112　twice

la ramita, la varilla

3113　twig

los gemelos, los mellizos

3114　twins

Las estrellas parpadean en el firmamento.

3115　Stars twinkle.

dar vueltas, hacer girar

3116　to twirl

torcer, retorcer

3117　to twist

dos

3118　two

Papá escribe a máquina todo el santo día.

3119　to type

la máquina de escribir

3120　typewriter

U

Medusa era **fea** pero tenía un no sé qué . . .

3121 ugly

el paraguas

3122 umbrella

el tío

El hermano de mamá es uno de mis **tíos**.
Mi otro **tío** es el hermano de papá.

My uncle is my mother's brother.
My other uncle is my father's brother.

3123 uncle

bajo, debajo de, menor de

Yo no voy **bajo** ninguna circunstancia.
Marisol se escondió **debajo de** las sábanas.
Los niños **menores de** 5 años no pueden ir.

I am not going under any circumstances.
Marisol is hiding under the covers.
Children under 5 cannot go.

3124 under

entender, comprender

3125 to understand

la ropa interior

3126 underwear

desvestirse, desnudarse

3127 to undress

triste, desconsolada, descontenta

3128 unhappy

Mi **unicornio** azul ayer se me perdió . . .

3129 unicorn

El coronel Buendía usaba **uniforme** de gala.

3130 uniform

la universidad

3131 university

descargar

3132 to unload

abrir la cerradura

3133 to unlock

desenvolver, desempaquetar

3134 to unwrap

derecho, vertical, enhiesto

3135 upright

al revés, patas arriba

3136 upside-down

Mamá **usa** pimienta para cocinar.

3137 to use

Usó tanta que la **gastó** toda.

3138 to use up

Este cortaplumas es muy **útil**.

3139 useful

Para Vigo me voy de vacaciones.

3140 vacation/holiday*

el vapor

3141 vapor/vapour*

Ismael barniza su escritorio.

3142 to varnish

el jarrón, el florero

3143 vase

un filete de **ternera**

3144 veal

las verduras, las legumbres, las hortalizas

3145 vegetable

Un coche es **un vehículo.**

3146 vehicle

Dulcinea se cubre la cara con **un velo.**

3147 veil

la vena

3148 vein

el veneno, la ponzoña

No todas las serpientes tienen **veneno.**
Algunos insectos tienen un veneno llamado **ponzoña.**

Not all snakes have venom.
Some insects have a poison called venom.

3149 venom

La vertical es lo contrario de la horizontal.

3150 vertical

muy, mismo, sumamente

Marisol opina que su hermano es **muy** ingenioso.
Estamos en el centro **mismo** de la ciudad.
Este un libro **sumamente** interesante.

Marisol thinks her brother is very clever.
We are in the very heart of the city.
This is a very interesting book.

3151 very

el chaleco

3152 vest/waistcoat*

Los veterinarios trabajan como animales.

3153 veterinarian/veterinary surgeon*

He aquí **la víctima** del crimen.

3154 victim

un aparato de video

3155 video recorder

Las cintas de vídeo se deben manejar con cuidado.

3156 video tape

la vista

Queremos un cuarto con **vista** al mar.
Todos tenemos nuestro propio punto de **vista.**

We would like a room with a view of the sea.
We each have our own point of view.

3157 view

el pueblo, la aldea

3158 village

el malhechor, el bandido, el villano

3159   villain

Las uvas nacen de **la vid**.

3160   vine

A Marisol le gusta **el vinagre**.

3161   vinegar

Cómpreme usted este ramito de **violetas** . . .

3162   violet

el violín

3163   violin

Para entrar a un país se necesita **una visa**.

3164   visa

visible

Han habido **visibles** cambios en la situación. Invisible es lo contrario de **visible**.

There have been visible changes in the situation. Invisible is the opposite of visible.

3165   visible

Matías fue a **visitar** a su tía al hospital.

3166   to visit

la visera

3167   visor

el vocabulario

El que tiene un buen **vocabulario** conoce muchas palabras. Tener un buen **vocabulario** es muy importante. Este diccionario te ayuda a agrandar tu **vocabulario**.

Someone who has a good vocabulary knows many words. A good vocabulary is very important. This dictionary helps increase your vocabulary.

3168   vocabulary

¡Qué buena **voz** tiene!

3169   voice

el volcán

3170   volcano

el vóleibol, la pelota de vóleibol

3171   volleyball

la voluntaria

3172   volunteer

vomitar

3173   to vomit

votar

3174   to vote

el votante

3175   voter

la vocal

Las **vocales** del alfabeto son la a, e, i, o y u.

A, E, I, O, U and Y are the only vowels in the alphabet.

3176   vowel

una larga **travesía** por mar.

3177   voyage

Los buitres comen carroña.

3178   vulture

W

Manuel se metió **chapoteando** al agua.
3179   to wade

el wafle, el barquillo
3180   waffle

la carreta, el carro, el carretón
3181   wagon/cart*

chillar, aullar, llorar, lamentarse
3182   to wail

una cintura de avispa
3183   waist

Antonia **aguarda** el autobús.
3184   to wait

¡Siempre me **despiertan** antes de tiempo!
3185   to wake

caminar, andar
3186   to walk

la pared, el muro, la muralla
3187   wall

la billetera, la cartera
3188   wallet

mucho ruido y pocas **nueces**
3189   walnut

la morsa
3190   walrus

la varita mágica de Merlín
3191   wand

vagar, errar
3192   to wander

querer, necesitar
¿Quién **quiere** más cereal?
Él letrero dice: "Se **necesitan** albañiles".
Marisol **quiere** lavar los platos pero no hay agua.

Who wants more cereal?
The sign says: "Bricklayers wanted".
Marisol wants to do the dishes but there is no water.
3193   to want

Marisol y sus amigos odian **la guerra**.
3194   war

el vestuario, la ropa
3195   wardrobe

la bodega, el almacén, el depósito
3196   warehouse

abrigado
3197   warm

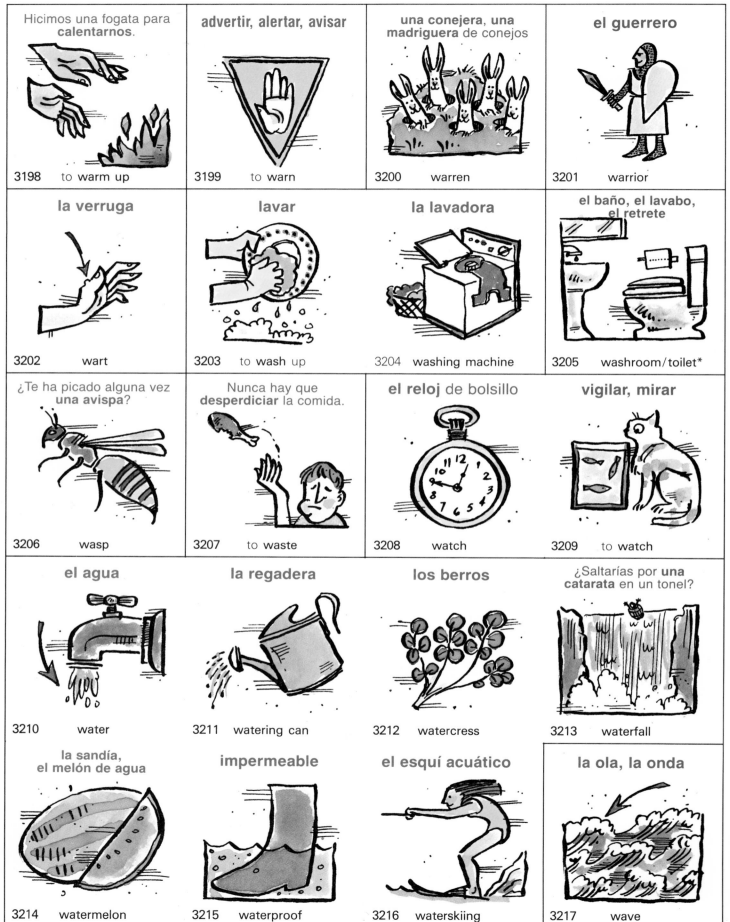

Hicimos una fogata para **calentarnos**.

3198   to **warm** up

advertir, alertar, avisar

3199   to **warn**

una **conejera**, una **madriguera** de conejos

3200   **warren**

el guerrero

3201   **warrior**

la verruga

3202   **wart**

lavar

3203   to **wash** up

la lavadora

3204   **washing** machine

el baño, el lavabo, el retrete

3205   **washroom/toilet***

¿Te ha picado alguna vez **una avispa**?

3206   **wasp**

Nunca hay que **desperdiciar** la comida.

3207   to **waste**

el reloj de bolsillo

3208   **watch**

vigilar, mirar

3209   to **watch**

el agua

3210   **water**

la regadera

3211   **watering** can

los berros

3212   **watercress**

¿Saltarías por **una catarata** en un tonel?

3213   **waterfall**

la sandía, el melón de agua

3214   **watermelon**

impermeable

3215   **waterproof**

el esquí acuático

3216   **waterskiing**

la ola, la onda

3217   **wave**

Verónica les **hace señas** a sus amigos.

3218   to **wave**

Ella tiene el cabello **ondulado**.

3219   **wavy**

Las velas están hechas de **cera**.

3220   **wax**

débil, enclenque

3221   **weak**

Las armas son muy peligrosas.

3222   **weapon**

llevar, ponerse, vestir, traer puesto

3223   to **wear**

la comadreja

3224   **weasel**

¿Cómo está **el tiempo** afuera?

3225   **weather**

tejer, trenzar, urdir, tramar, entrelazar

3226   to **weave**

Los patos tienen patas **palmeadas**.

3227   **web foot**

la boda, el casamiento, el matrimonio

3228   **wedding**

la cuña

3229   **wedge**

el miércoles

El **miércoles** es el tercer día de la semana.
Marisol saca la basura **los miércoles**.

*Wednesday is the third day of the week.
On Wednesdays, Marisol takes out the garbage.*

3230   **Wednesday**

Los mejores jardines tienen **malezas**.

3231   **weed**

La semana tiene siete días.

3232   **week**

el fin de semana

Tía Mercedes viene de visita este **fin de semana**.
El **fin de semana** es el sábado y el domingo.
El hombre del tiempo dijo que llovería este **fin de semana**.

*Aunt Mercedes will visit us this weekend.
Saturday and Sunday make a weekend.
The weatherman says it will rain this weekend.*

3233   **weekend**

La gente **llora** cuando está triste.

3234   to **weep**

pesar

3235   to **weigh**

un tipo **extraño**

3236   **weird**

Dolores le **dio la bienvenida** a su amiga.

3237   to **welcome**

el pozo de agua

3238   well

¡Me siento muy bien!

3239   I feel well.

Cuando el norte está arriba, el oeste queda a la izquierda.

3240   west

mojado, empapado

3241   wet

¡No hay que dejar que las ballenas se extingan!

3243   whale

el muelle, el malecón, el embarcadero

3244   wharf

qué, lo que

¿**Qué** le pasó al pobre Micifuz?
Marisol, ¿**qué** le has hecho a tu gato?
Marisol, ¿escuchas **lo que** te digo?

What happened to poor Micifuz?
Marisol, what did you do to your cat?
Marisol, did you hear what I said?

3245   what

mojar, empapar

3242   to wet

el trigo

3246   wheat

la rueda

3247   wheel

la carretilla

3248   wheelbarrow

la silla de ruedas

3249   wheelchair

cuándo, cuando

¿**Cuándo** vendrá tía Mercedes, papá?
Cuando llegue el fin de semana.
¿Y **cuándo** será eso?

When is Aunt Mercedes coming, Dad?
When the weekend starts.
When is that?

3250   when

dónde, donde, adónde

Nos perdimos y mamá no tiene idea en **dónde** estamos.
Este es el lugar **donde** yo nací.
¿**Adónde** vamos?

We are lost and Mom has no idea where we are.
This is the place where I was born.
Where are we going?

3251   where

¿Cuál de los tres?

3252   which one

gimotear, quejarse

3253   to whine

el látigo

3254   whip

un ave llamada chotacabras

3255   whippoorwill

el batidor

3256   whisk

Micifuz tiene unos largos bigotes.

3257   whisker

Marisol le **susurró** un secreto a su amiga.

3258   to whisper

el pito, el silbato

3259   whistle

silbar, chiflar

3260   to whistle

el color blanco

3261   white

¿Quién de ustedes viene?

3262   Who is going?

por qué, cómo es que

Lo que yo quiero saber es **por qué** Marisol tomó mi corbata.
¿Cómo es que ella no se acuerda?

I want to know why Marisol took my tie.
Why can she not remember?

3263   why

Las lámparas antiguas tenían **mecha**.

3264   wick

un tipo **malvado**

3265   wicked

ancha, amplia

3266   wide

la esposa, la mujer, la señora

3267   wife

El león es un animal **salvaje**.

3268   The lion is a wild animal.

el sauce llorón

3269   willow

Las flores **se marchitan** si no las riegan.

3270   to wilt

taimado, ladino, astuto

3271   wily

ganar

3272   to win

respingar, recular, encogerse

3273   to wince

el viento

3274   wind

dar cuerda

3275   to wind

una chaqueta **cortaviento**

3276   windbreaker

¡No son gigantes, mi señor, son **molinos de viento**!

3277   windmill

la ventana

3278   window

el parabrisas

3279   windshield/windscreen*

El vino es para que lo beban los grandes.

3280   wine

el ala

3281   wing

El búho sabio te **guiña** un ojo.

3282   to wink

el invierno

3283   winter

limpiar, frotar

3284   to wipe

Este es **un alambre** eléctrico.

3285   wire

sabio, prudente

Mi abuelo es un hombre sabio.
¿Tú crees que sea **prudente** que Marisol camine sola por el bosque?

Grandfather is a wise old man. Do you think that it is wise for Marisol to walk in the forest alone?

3286   wise

pedir **un deseo**

3287   to make a wish

la bruja

3288   witch

el mago, el brujo, el hechicero

3289   wizard

¡Que viene **el lobo**!

3290   wolf

un hombre y **una mujer**

3291   woman

tener curiosidad, querer saber, preguntarse

3292   to wonder

maravilloso

3293   wonderful

la leña, la madera

3294   wood

Los pájaros carpinteros se alimentan de insectos.

3295   woodpecker

el bosque

3296   woods

el tallado en madera, la carpintería

3297   woodwork

Este es un ovillo de **lana**.

3298 wool

¡Pero qué **palabra** más rara!

GLÜRP

3299 word

En la vida nada se hace sin **trabajo**.

3300 work

trabajar, laborar

3301 to work

el taller

3303 workshop

El mundo, ni más ni menos.

3304 world

el gusano, la lombriz

3305 worm

hacer ejercicio

3302 to work out

Mamá **se preocupa** mucho por Marisol.

3306 to worry

la herida, la lesión

3307 wound

envolver

3308 to wrap

la corona de flores

3309 wreath

el naufragio

3310 wreck

el reyezuelo

3311 wren

luchar

3312 to wrestle

estrujar, retorcer, exprimir

3313 to wring

Con esta **muñeca** no se juega.

3314 wrist

el reloj de pulsera

3315 wristwatch

escribir

3316 to write

equivocado, malo, incorrecto

Yo creo que este autobús va en dirección **equivocada**.
Yo sé distinguir entre lo bueno y lo **malo**.
Esta dirección es **incorrecta**.

I think our bus is going the wrong way.
I know the difference between right and wrong.
This is the wrong address.

3317 wrong

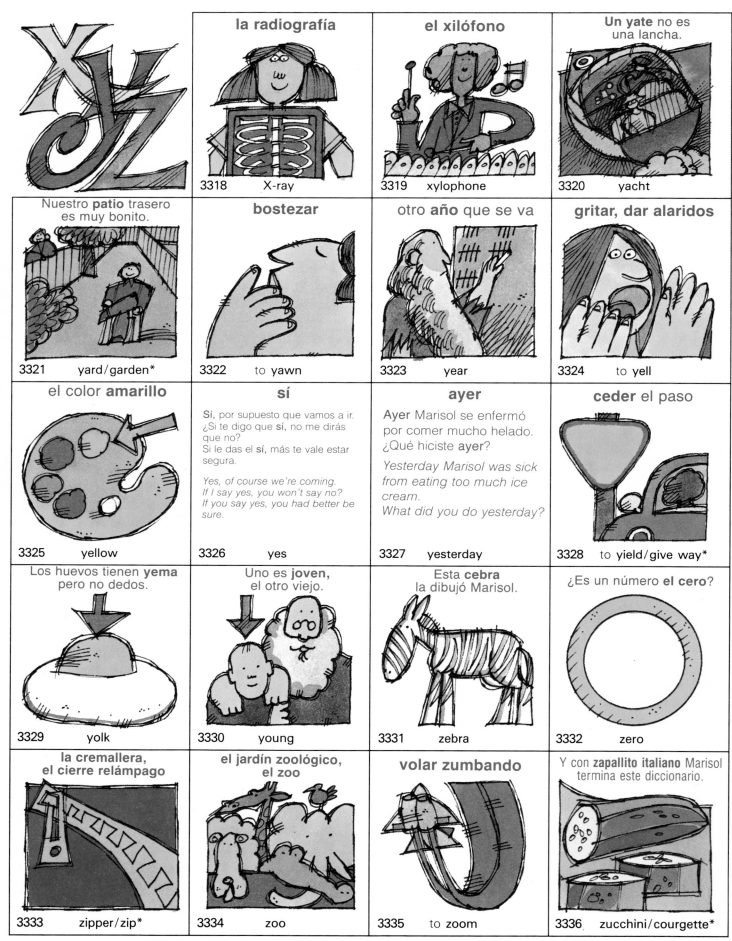

la radiografía

3318 X-ray

el xilófono

3319 xylophone

Un yate no es una lancha.

3320 yacht

Nuestro **patio** trasero es muy bonito.

3321 yard/garden*

bostezar

3322 to yawn

otro **año** que se va

3323 year

gritar, dar alaridos

3324 to yell

el color **amarillo**

3325 yellow

sí

Sí, por supuesto que vamos a ir.
¿Si te digo que **sí**, no me dirás que no?
Si le das el **sí**, más te vale estar segura.

Yes, of course we're coming.
If I say yes, you won't say no?
If you say yes, you had better be sure.

3326 yes

ayer

Ayer Marisol se enfermó por comer mucho helado. ¿Qué hiciste **ayer**?

Yesterday Marisol was sick from eating too much ice cream.
What did you do yesterday?

3327 yesterday

ceder el paso

3328 to yield/give way*

Los huevos tienen **yema** pero no dedos.

3329 yolk

Uno es **joven**, el otro viejo.

3330 young

Esta **cebra** la dibujó Marisol.

3331 zebra

¿Es un número **el cero**?

3332 zero

la cremallera, **el cierre relámpago**

3333 zipper/zip*

el jardín zoológico, **el zoo**

3334 zoo

volar zumbando

3335 to zoom

Y con **zapallito italiano** Marisol termina este diccionario.

3336 zucchini/courgette*

a

a 1455
ábaco (el) 1
abadejo (el) 1235
abalanzarse 2216, 2898
abandonar 839
abarrotes (los) 1210
abatirse 2898
abeja (la) 216
abejera (la) 80
abeto (el) 996, 2777
abierto 1952
abofetear 2674
abollar 747
abordar 2906
abrazar 890
abrazarse 890
abrelatas (el) 418
abridor (el) 317
abrigado 3197
abrigo (el) 566, 1976
abril 88
abrir 1953
abrir la cerradura 3133
abrochar 960
abrocharse 960
abuela (la) 1182
abuelo (el) 1181
aburrir 311
acabar de 1510
acampar 415
acanaladura (la) 1214
acantilado (el) 543
acaparar 1341
acarrear 1279, 3057
acaso 1753
accidente (el) 7
acebo (el) 1353
acedera (la) 2730
acedía (la) 2138
aceite (el) 1942
aceituna (la) 1945
acelerador (el) 5, 1111
acelerar 2747
acelga (la) 491
acento (el) 6
acerca de 2
acercarse 86
acero (el) 2807

acezar 2013
acicalarse 1213
ácido 2734
ácido (el) 12
acordarse 2368, 2395
acordeón (el) 8
acostarse 1633
acróbata (el, la) 14
actuación (la) 2085
acuario (el) 90
acusar 9
adelante 1058
adelante de 33
además 239
además de 239
adiós 1168
adivinar 1223
adolorido 2729
adónde 3251
adorar 19
adornar 742
adorno (el) 743
adulto (el) 20
advertir 3199
aerodeslizador (el) 1390
aeropuerto (el) 40
a escala 1817
afeitar 2589
aferrarse 1260
afilado 2584
afilador (el) 2585, 2586
afortunado 1700
Africa 25
agacharse 2828
agalla (la) 1139
agarrar 459, 559, 1127,
    1207, 2560
agarrarse 1260
ágil 31
agitar 2579
agosto 126
agotarse 2478
agradable 2158
agradecer 2964
agrio 2734
agua (el) 3210
agua de lavar los platos
    (el) 786
aguacate (el) 133
aguanieve (el) 2696

aguardar 3184
aguijonear 2182
águila (el) 858
aguja (la) 1890, 2759
agujero (el) 1350
ahí 2967
ahogar 522
ahorrar 2508
aire (el) 36
aire libre (el) 1971
aislamiento (el) 1452
aislante (el) 1452
ají (el) 1385
ajo (el) 1107
al 117
al agua 1975
al lado de 238
al poco rato 2727
al revés 3136
ala (el) 3281
alabar 2224
alacena (la) 1409
alambrada de púas (la)
    169
alambre (el) 3285
álamo (el) 2197
alardear 2624
albahaca (la) 187
albañil (el) 344
albaricoque (el) 87
alberca (la) 2193
albergue (el) 1680
alboroto (el) 2328
álbum (el) 43
alcachofa (la) 104
alcalde (el) 1754
alcanzar 460, 2357
alce (el) 1833
aldea (la) 3158
alegre 1149, 1775
alerce (el) 1574
alertar 3199
aleta (la) 990
aletear 1014
alfabeto (el) 54
alfarería (la) 2214
alfombra (la) 446
alga (el) 2553
algodón (el) 636
alhaja (la) 1488

alicate (el) 2161
aliento (el) 341
aligerar 1640
alimentar 972
alimento (el) 1043
allá 2967
allí 2967
almacén (el) 2613, 2832,
    3196
almacenero (el) 1209,
    2614
almanaque (el) 407
almeja (la) 535
almendra (la) 49
almirante (el) 18
almohadón (el) 2119
almorzar 870
almuerzo (el) 1706
alondra (la) 1577, 2670
alquilar 2398
alquitrán (el) 2135, 2933
alrededor de 99
altavoz (el) 1693
altillo (el) 1681
altiplanicie (la) 2152
alto (el) 2829
alto 1328, 2921
altoparlante (el) 378
alumbrar 1426
aluminio (el) 58
alumno (el) 2856
alzar 1636
alzar en vilo 1297
amable 1529
amaestrar 3052
amapola (la) 2198
amargo 258
amarillo 3325
amarrar 250, 2997
ambos 315
ambulancia (la) 60
a menudo 1941
americana (la) 272
amiga (la) 1073
amígdala (la) 3022
amodorrado 840
amontonarse 1395
amor (el) 1695
amoroso 1697
amplio 3266

C

e

f

guarida (la) 1559
guerra (la) 3194
guerrero (el) 3201
guiar 2810
guijarro (el) 2065
guiñar 3282
guinda (la) 503
guineo (el) 160
guión (el) 1412
guisante (el) 2063
guitarra (la) 1228
gusano (el) 1710, 3305
gustar 1644

h

habichuela verde (la) 1199
habichuelas (las) 204
hábil 1258
habitación (la) 2452
habitar 1439
hablar 2745, 2920
hacer 796, 1719
hacer cariño 2093
hacer cosquillas 2994
hacer daño 1270
hacer ejercicio 920, 3302
hacer entrega 2231
hacer estallar 270
hacer gárgaras 1106
hacer girar 3116
hacer ostentación 2624
hacer pedazos 2699
hacer pucheros 2220
hacer señas 3218
hacer trampa 498
hacer un boceto 2660
hacer un borrón 2700
hacer un bosquejo 2660
hacer un croquis 2660
hacer un saludo 2496
hacer una pausa 2050
hacer volar 270
hacerse agua la boca 834
hacerse añicos 2588

hacha (el) 138
hachuela (la) 1278
hada (el) 942
halar 2277
halcón (el) 1282
Halloween 1243
hamaca (la) 1248
hámster (el) 1249
hangar (el) 1262
harapiento 2575
harina (la) 1030
haya (el) 217
haz de luz (el) 203
hebilla (la) 369
hechicero (el) 2728, 3289
hediondo 2702
helado (el) 1414
helado 512
helecho (el) 977
hélice (la) 2262
helicóptero (el) 1303·
hembra (la) 974
hemisferio (el) 1311
heno (el) 1283
heptágono (el) 1313
herida (la) 361, 1442, 3307
hermana (la) 2652
hermano (el) 358
hermético 38
hermoso 209, 1171
héroe (el) 1318
heroína (la) 1319
herradura (la) 1380
herramienta (la) 3023
herrero (el) 264
hervir 301
hexágono (el) 1322
hibernar 1323
hiedra (la) 1471
hielo (el) 1413
hierba (la) 1188, 1314
hierbabuena (la) 1800
hierro (el) 1466
hija (la) 734
hijo (el) 2725
hilacha (la) 1657
hilo (el) 2980
himno (el) 1411
hincarse 1541

hipar 1324
hipocampo (el) 2543
hipopótamo (el) 1337
historia (la) 1338
hockey (el) 1344
hogar (el) 1002
hogaza (la) 1673
hoguera (la) 304
hoja (la) 265, 1599
hola 1305
holgazán 1596
holgazanear 1694
hombre (el) 1723
hombro (el) 2619
honda (la) 2687
hondonada (la) 2353
hongo (el) 1861
honrado 1357
hora (la) 1387, 3002
horadar 310
horizontal 1373
horizonte (el) 1372
hormiga (la) 71
hornear 149
horno (el) 1524, 1974
horquilla (la) 299, 2134
hortaliza (la) 3145
hospital (el) 1382
hotel (el) 1386
hoy 3012
hoy día 3012
hoyo (el) 1350
hoyuelo (el) 769
hueco (el) 1101
hueco 1352
huelga (la) 2851
huellas dactilares (las) 994
huellas digitales (las) 994
huérfano (el) 1967
huerta (la) 1105
huerto (el) 1960
hueso (el) 303
huésped (el) 1224
huevo (el) 876
huir 1023, 2476
húmedo 725
humor (el) 1830
hundirse 2649

huracán (el) 1404

i

idea (la) 1418
idéntico 1419
idioma (el) 1571
idiota (el) 1420
iglú (el) 1423
igual 904, 2497
iluminar 1426
ilustración (la) 1427
imán (el) 1713
impedimento (el) 1254
impermeable (el) 2339
impermeable 3215
implorar 2157
importante 1428
importunar 2091
imprimir 2245
inactivo 1421
incendio (el) 271, 997
incienso (el) 1430
inclinado 2673
inclinarse 1601
incorrecto 3317
indefenso 1309
indicar 2639
índice (el) 1432
indicio (el) 557
índigo (el) 1433
indumentaria (la) 1972
infección (la) 1436
infeccioso 1437
infierno (el) 1304
influenza (la) 1033
inicial (la) 1440
iniciarse 224
inmundo 989
inodoro (el) 3015
inscribir 2387
inscribirse 2387
insecto (el) 1444
insignia (la) 146
insistir 1446
inspeccionar 1447
inspector (el) 1448
instrucciones (las) 1450

S

té (el) 2941
teatro (el) 1851, 2966
techo (el) 467, 2451
teja (la) 2601
tejer 1543, 3226
tejo de hockey (el) 1345
tela (la) 550
telar (el) 1687
telaraña (la) 567
telefonear 411, 2951
teléfono (el) 2099, 2950
teléfono público (el) 2054
telegrama (el) 2949
telescopio (el) 2952
televisión (la) 2953
temblar 2322, 2607, 3066
témpano (el) 1415
temperatura (la) 2956
tempestad (la) 2834
tempestad de nieve (la) 279
temprano 860
tenaza (la) 2123, 3019
tendedero (el) 552
tendero (el) 2614
tenedor (el) 1054
tener 1281, 1982
tener curiosidad 3292
tener hambre 1401
tener hipo 1324
tener la culpa 266
tener miedo 968
tener que 1865
tener sueño 2680
tenis (el) 2958, 2959
tercero 2976
terminal (el) 2962
terminar 995
termómetro (el) 2968
ternera (la) 3144
ternero (el) 408
terno (el) 2865
terremoto (el) 864
tesoro (el) 3064
tetera (la) 1516, 2945
tía (la) 127
tibio 1702
tiburón (el) 2583

tiempo (el) 3225
tienda (la) 2613, 2832
tienda de campaña (la) 2960
tierra (la) 863, 1216, 1566
Tierra (la) 862
tieso 2818
tigre (el) 2998
tijeras (las) 2528
tijeras de podar (las) 2590
tímido 2633
timón (el) 1306, 2468
tina (la) 194, 3092
tinta (la) 1443
tío (el) 3123
tipo (el) 1528
tirabuzón (el) 628
tirador (el) 805, 2687
tirante (el) 2842
tirantes (los) 2883
tirar 2277, 2612, 2986
tirar de 3095
tiritar 2607
tiro (el) 2133
títere (el) 2289
titubear 1321
tiza (la) 483
toalla (la) 3039
tobillo (el) 67
tobogán (el) 2683
tocadiscos (el) 2374
tocar 208, 3036
tocar el timbre 2426
tocar la bocina 1361
tocino (el) 144
tocón (el) 2859
todo 46, 914
tomacorriente (el) 2718
tomar 829, 2910
tomar asiento 2653
tomar el desayuno 869
tomar prestado 313
tomate (el) 3016
tomillo (el) 2992
tonelada (la) 3021
tono (el) 2133
tonto 2643
topo (el) 1820

torcer 3117
torcerse 2769
torcido 675, 676
tormenta (la) 2834
tormenta eléctrica (la) 2990
tornado (el) 3032
tornillo (el) 2539
toro (el) 375
toronja (la) 1186
torpe 137
torre (la) 3040
torrecilla (la) 3108
torrente (el) 3033
torreta (la) 3108
torta (la) 405
tortilla (la) 1946
tortuga (la) 3034, 3109
tosco 564
toser 638
tostada (la) 3010
tostadora (la) 3011
traba (la) 181
trabajar 3301
trabajo (el) 1490, 3300
tractor (el) 3045
traer 351
traer puesto 3223
tráfico (el) 3047
tragar 2884
trago (el) 828
traílla (la) 1603
traje (el) 634, 2865
tramar 3226
trampa (la) 3059
trampolín (el) 3055
tranquilo 2316
transatlántico (el) 1654
transbordador (el) 978
transparente 3056
transpirar 2888
transportador (el) 3058
transportar 3057
trapecio (el) 3060
tras 26
trasero (el) 2363
tratar 3091
travesía (la) 3177
trébol (el) 554
tren (el) 3051

trenzar 3226
tres 2982
triángulo (el) 3069
triciclo (el) 3072
trigo (el) 3246
trinchar 452
trineo (el) 2677
tripulación (la) 668
triste 2485, 3128
triturar 686, 2218
trocar 2886, 3046
trole (el) 3077
trolebús (el) 3077
trompa (la) 3088
trompeta (la) 3085
trompo (el) 3029
tronada (la) 2990
tronco (el) 1682, 3087
trono (el) 2985
tropezar 3076
trotar 1492, 3078
trozo (el) 529
trucha (la) 3081
truco (el) 3070
trueno (el) 2989
tubo (el) 3093
tubo respiratorio (el) 2711
tulipán (el) 3096
tumba (la) 1191, 3017
túnel (el) 3098
tupido 2969
turba (la) 2064
turquesa 3107

u

u 1957
ufanarse 297
último 1579
umbral (el) 2983
uña (la) 1869
una vez 1948
unguento (el) 1943
único 1951
unicornio (el) 3129
uniforme (el) 3130
unir 122